SOCIAL SECURITY SIMPLIFIED

A COMPREHENSIVE GUIDE TO MAXIMIZE YOUR
BENEFITS, UNDERSTAND YOUR OPTIONS, AND
SECURE YOUR RETIREMENT FOR FINANCIAL
INDEPENDENCE

RETIREWISE

TABLE OF CONTENTS

INTRODUCTION

Is the idea of applying for Social Security confusing or overwhelming for you? If you're like most people, you might not know much about it and may be afraid that you'll make a mistake that'll ultimately cost you a LOT of money.

It can be easy to leave money on the table if you're unsure what you're doing, especially if you have a less-than-straightforward situation. Many people get confused about the rules when it comes to what ex-spouses are entitled to, when the best time to apply for retirement benefits is, or what program you should be applying to.

Just imagine what you could do with that money! You could pay off your mortgage (if you haven't already), buy a new car, or just be generous with your gifts to your children or grandchildren.

Most people miss out because they can't navigate the complex Social Security system and assume they are getting what they're supposed to get. But that's not you! You picked up this book because trying to get your Social Security benefits was like walking through a hedge maze blindfolded, and you wanted to ensure you understood the system.

That's what we're going to explore together in the pages of this book. By the time you finish reading this guide, you'll have a far better handle on what Social Security is, all of its benefits, and how to claim every last penny you are *rightly* entitled to.

SHORTCUTS TO SUCCESS

It would take years to learn each and every detail of Social Security. Fortunately, with this guide in your pocket, you won't need to.

Instead, in the coming chapters, you'll learn exactly what you need to know:

- **How to maximize your benefits:** You'll learn about all the factors that can impact your benefit amount and how to get the most possible money from Social Security.
- **How to make an informed choice about Medicare:** Medicare plans can be confusing. You'll learn how to choose a plan that fits your healthcare needs better, and can save you the most money on needed services each year.
- **How to budget for extra health care costs:** Some healthcare costs may not be covered by Medicare, but there are still ways to save money. You'll learn how to plan ahead and save for these costs.
- **Insights into government pensions:** Social Security may not be the only government pension you're entitled to. You'll learn about all available pension plans and how to take advantage of them.

- **Comprehensive retirement planning:** You won't be stuck working, when you're more than ready to retire, if you learn how to plan for your golden years. Social Security is an important, but not the only, aspect of this plan.
- **How to avoid common traps:** You'll learn about the more common mistakes people make that lose them money, and how to sidestep these traps.
- **Stress reduction:** You'll learn how to plan your finances so that you're not stressed out as you approach retirement, or after you've already stopped working.
- **Save time and energy:** Theoretically, you could read a ton of books about Social Security or retirement planning, but that'll sap your energy and take a long time to complete. Instead, you can learn everything you need to know in one fell swoop with just this book.

THE MOST IMPORTANT STEP YOU CAN TAKE

If you want a successful retirement, the most important thing to do for yourself is plan for it. Retirement is both an exciting and a scary time for many people. If you've planned properly, you'll have a solid foundation: a nest egg you can draw upon to support yourself and your family and live the life of your dreams. However, poor planning makes this impossible; you could run out of money or be unable to afford to retire at all!

Retirement planning doesn't just involve how much money you'll need to achieve your goals. While you are still working, you'll need to put some money away for retirement. It's helpful to understand the different types of retirement plans. In addition, you'll need to know the basics so that you don't risk money unnecessarily or make any bad investments that waste your hard-earned cash before you're ready to retire.

As you can see, retirement planning is complicated. But it's worth it for several reasons (Foneville, n.d.):

- **You don't know what you don't know:** Sure, you could learn through trial and error, but mistakes you make with retirement planning could get extremely costly. It's better to learn about retirement plans and set something up for the future NOW than waking up later to realize you had an expensive blind spot.
- **Reducing stress is good for your health:** Many people live 25 or more years past retirement, but extra stress can shorten your post-retirement lifespan considerably. Stress can cause heart disease and has been implicated in the development of cancer. By planning ahead, you'll have less financial stress, and in turn, enjoy better health during your golden years.
- **Proper planning saves you on taxes:** The less you pay in taxes, the more money you have to enjoy! But to fully take advantage of tax savings, you need to know what the rules are and how to plan your finances to take advantage of them.
- **Make better career and financial decisions:** It's hard to consider your long-term interests if you don't have a plan. Rather than planning day by day or paycheck-by-paycheck, use a retirement plan to help you identify and prepare for the next step in your career and your eventual retirement.
- **Provide for your children:** Nobody wants to think that they will be a burden to their children during their old age

or that their kids will be stuck under a mountain of debt after they die. Retirement planning ensures that won't happen.

- **Be the grandparent you've always wanted to be:** Spoiling grandchildren and taking them on special outings is half the fun of being a grandparent! You'll need good money to do these things, so plan for your retirement so that you can be that "ultra-cool" grandma or grandpa!
- **Continue (or begin) giving to charity:** Many people want to leave behind a legacy that includes charitable giving. If you have a cause you're passionate about, you'll want to plan your retirement accordingly so that you can give both time and money to it.

WHY AND HOW RETIREWISE CAN HELP

This book is one way we can help people like you to live the life of their dreams after retirement. We've gathered all the information you need to get started on your retirement planning in one place, offering you facts and ideas that you won't find anywhere else.

The reason that people fail to plan adequately for retirement is that they don't know how to go about it. Websites and Google searches can get you basic information about Social Security or retirement plans, but they only go so far. In these pages, we share secrets that most people don't know—information that will allow you to maximize your savings and live far more comfortably than you might have thought possible. And that's what we want for every reader: a life well lived... both before and after retirement.

LET'S GET STARTED!

Retirement planning can make the *real* difference between living a full, happy life and being miserable. For example, before reading this book, some people had to consider taking a part-time job after retirement or delaying retirement, and are now being able to live fully and freely, giving donations to their favorite charities and spending more quality time with their children and grandchildren.

That could be you, too.

Social Security and other aspects of retirement planning can be confusing, but reading this book will change that for you. Retire-Wise has helped hundreds of people like you to set and achieve financial goals so that you can live a post-retirement life that exceeds your wildest dreams.

Retirement can, and should be, an exciting adventure. Turn the page and let's get started!

1

SOCIAL SECURITY DECIPHERED - YOUR STARTING POINT FOR RETIREMENT PLANNING

A re you using Social Security for at least some of your bills? If so, you're not alone. Social Security makes up 49% of income for people over the age of 65, and for about a quarter of people your age, it makes up a whopping 90% of your income (SSA, 2017). Although this program is an extremely important part of financial planning for most older Americans, most people have limited understanding of how it works.

Let's change that in this chapter. We'll start by discussing the principles this program is based on, including its purposes and how it's paid for. Once you understand this, we can discuss how Social Security benefits can help you create the retirement of your dreams.

THE BASICS: HOW, WHEN, AND WHY TO USE SOCIAL SECURITY

As you may know, the original Social Security program was instituted in 1935—at the height of the Great Depression. It's considered one of President Franklin D. Roosevelt's (FDR) flagship accomplishments; we'll discuss the history later on, but first let's look at the program's purposes, how it is funded, and what it doesn't do.

FDR envisioned a society where the government helped take care of its senior citizens. After the widespread economic troubles of the Great Depression, he became aware that family support or help from charity wasn't a given; he wanted to ensure that everyone could afford to retire once they reached the appropriate age to do so (today, the retirement age is 67, although you can begin taking Social Security benefits as early as 62).

Social Security also protects two other classes of people:

- Those who cannot work because of a disabling condition.
- Those who lose significant income because of the death of a spouse.

Although today, many politicians call Social Security a type of welfare program, that's not accurate—working people fund the program via payroll taxes, so the benefits you get revolve partially around how much you paid into it. These taxes are mandatory; employers deduct them before you get your paycheck, and if you have your own business. you pay double (your taxes and those of your employees').

The program is based on several principles:

Principle 1: Protection is Universal

In order to reduce poverty, Social Security tries to distribute resources equitably (Ball, 1998). Relatedly, Social Security is a universal program. If you are a US citizen or permanent resident, you have the right to claim Social Security benefits.

In contrast, programs like SNAP benefits are "means-tested," which means you have to be low-income to qualify for them. Social Security does not have this rule. The only requirement is that you are at the right age to begin claiming benefits. And like all government programs, discrimination against members of protected classes, in terms of race and age, is strictly prohibited.

Principle 2: Everyone Pays Into the System

Your benefits are based on your earnings over a 35-year period (We discuss this in detail later in the book). Thus, Social Security is not the type of program where everyone's tax dollars go to a few people; your taxes fund your Social Security benefits. Think of Social Security as a type of government pension. You get what you pay into it.

Principle 3: Benefits are Adjusted to Create Equity

In general, as mentioned above, higher wages lead to higher benefits. However, there is a built-in equity factor. If wages were the only consideration, low-income workers might not get enough benefits to live off of. Thus, their benefits are adjusted to ensure they receive enough after retirement to support themselves.

Principle 4: Social Security Is Not Paid for by Deficit Spending

Politicians who are looking to cut social programs to save money sometimes suggest that Social Security costs too much. However, Social Security is not financed by income taxes; each worker pays into it. These employee contributions means that the program doesn't contribute to federal deficits, and cutting it won't help reduce the national debt. In addition, since workers pay for the program, it's unfair not to give it to them. Workers generally are against excessive cuts to Social Security for this reason, but may not want large increases in benefits either—this would mean contributing a larger percentage of their paychecks to Social Security taxes.

Principle 5: Social Security Benefits Follow You if You Change Jobs

Social Security benefits don't disappear if you change jobs—this would otherwise defeat the purpose of the program. Instead, the Social Security Administration keeps track of all of your earnings and payments into the system so that you receive benefits based on your top 35 years of earnings, regardless of how often you've changed jobs.

Principle 6: Social Security Takes Current Economic Conditions Into Account

35 years is a long time, and in many cases, your wages—when you began—aren't worth much now because of inflation. Social Security takes this into account; wages are adjusted for inflation before benefits are calculated to ensure you're getting enough money to support yourself in the current economy. In addition, the SSA occasionally raises benefit amounts to reflect higher costs of living. That way, you won't fall short of what you need if groceries,

gas, and other necessities become more expensive because of inflation.

Principle 7: You Can't Opt Out of Paying for Social Security

One of the reasons the SSA uses payroll taxes to fund its activities is to ensure that everyone pays their fair share. Neither bosses nor employees have a choice; they have to pay payroll taxes. This ensures that Social Security will never run out of money and that people who object on principle can't refuse to contribute.

WHAT EXACTLY IS SOCIAL SECURITY?

If you're still a bit confused about exactly what Social Security is, don't panic! The principles we outlined above will make more sense once we've discussed more fully what the program is and isn't.

Most people know Social Security as a program for senior citizens. But, in actuality, Social Security comprises several different programs:

- Retirement benefits for those aged 62 or older
- Survivors' benefits for those who have lost their spouse
- Disability benefits for those who are unable to work because of permanent disability.

If you have a disabled child, you may also be eligible for benefits on their behalf until they turn 18.

All three programs are run by the Social Security Administration; the full name of the Social Security program is "Old Age, Survivors, and Disability Insurance Program," or OASDI. Approximately, 67 million people will receive benefits from one or more of these programs in 2023 (Connett, 2023).

PURPOSES OF SOCIAL SECURITY

Social Security was created with several purposes in mind:

- **To provide for families:** During the Great Depression, it became clear that people might need government assistance to provide for themselves, often because of events that were beyond their control. Thus, Social Security was created to provide a safety net for families that might experience hardship because of death or disability. In addition, Social Security created a retirement pension program to ensure that senior citizens could live comfortably in their golden years, regardless of economic conditions.

- **To help offset the cost of health care for vulnerable populations:** Both older people and those who are disabled may have medical conditions that require frequent doctor visits or expensive treatments. Thus, the Social Security Administration offers Medicare to ensure that those who are eligible have their healthcare needs duly covered.

- **To keep families together:** If it weren't for Social Security, some people might not be able to provide adequately for their children or might need to go out of state for work, leaving their children and families behind. In addition, families with a disabled member may need some extra-help caring for that member at home rather than placing them in a facility. Thus, Social Security benefits can help keep families together.

- **To give children equal opportunity to grow up in healthy, secure situations:** Survivor and disability benefits help ensure that children, who live in a home where a parent has passed away or someone is disabled, exercise the same opportunity to live healthy lives like children from more affluent homes.

WHAT PROGRAMS EXIST UNDER SOCIAL SECURITY?

The Social Security Administration (SSA) oversees many programs. In addition to the three main programs (Retirement, Disability, and Survivor benefits), the SSA offers a wide range of government-funded programs to help people:

- Help with health care needs, such as Medicare and Prescription Drug Coverage programs for eligible people
- Veterans' Benefits
- Supplemental Security Income for those with disabilities or who have extremely low income
- Unemployment Insurance
- Temporary aid for those in need, including:

  - Temporary assistance for families
  - Medical assistance
  - Maternal and child health services
  - Child support services
  - Parent and child welfare services
  - Food stamps
  - Energy assistance

In most cases, self-employed individuals are also covered by Social Security—in fact, 9 out of 10 workers, whether they work at a job or own their own business, are covered. Self-employed people pay their own Social Security taxes based on their yearly earnings as well as the taxes for any employees they hire and pay during the year.

Throughout this book, we will concentrate mainly on the "big three" programs (Retirement, Survivors, and Disability) as well as Medicare and other healthcare benefits. But, as you can see, Social Security offers many benefits to those in need! If you or your family are ever in dire straits, keep in mind that there is help available.

THE STRUCTURE OF THE SOCIAL SECURITY ADMINISTRATION

The Social Security Administration has both a central office and a number of local offices. The central office is located in Baltimore, Maryland.

While not every town has a local office, many towns and cities do. If you don't have a local office in your immediate vicinity, you may have one a few towns over. Hopefully, your local office is only a few minutes away by car or bus! It's important to find out where your local office is because this is where you will do most of your business. Local Social Security offices offer most of these services:

- Applications for new Social Security numbers or replacement Social Security cards
- Applications for any benefits you need, such as retirement or survivor benefits, healthcare coverage, or disability benefits
- Enrolling in Medicare or other healthcare coverage programs

- Assistance with applying for food stamps or other welfare programs
- Information about how much you've paid into the program and what your benefits should be
- Information about your rights and those of your family to Social Security benefits

These services are all free of charge; you will never have to pay to receive information, assistance, or benefits at a local Social Security office.

The Social Security Administration also has 10 regional offices that oversee all the local areas in a given region. Finally, there are teleservice offices in major cities throughout the United States. These offices field telephone calls and refer people to the correct local or regional office to take care of their needs.

HOW TO APPLY FOR SOCIAL SECURITY BENEFITS

You can fill out your application online, though you may have to mail some supporting documents. You can also apply over the phone or in person at your local SSA office.

If you aren't sure where your local office is, there are two ways to find out: (1) You can use the online [SSA Office Locator] (https://secure.ssa.gov/apps6z/FOLO/fo001.jsp) or (2) call the SSA at 1-800-772-1213 between the hours of 7 a.m. and 7 p.m. EST. This number is toll-free, so you won't be charged for your call.

In some cases, the nearest Social Security office may be too far away for you to get to easily. If you're in this situation, the Social Security Administration offers visits to specified locations called "contact stations." You can get this information from the phone number listed above. If you can't find a convenient location, you can also arrange for a representative to visit your home.

Finally, you can apply for benefits via telephone using the 800 number.

IT'S IMPORTANT TO KEEP UP WITH YOUR BENEFITS

Social Security coverage is extremely important. Not only can it be a vital part of your retirement plan, but it can also offer support to you and your family in dire and unforeseen circumstances.

About three months before your birthday each year, you should receive a statement in the mail listing your Social Security benefits. If you do not receive this statement, or you have any questions about benefit amounts, contact your local office. You should also contact your relevant employer if you don't see your job listed on your statement.

ARE GOVERNMENT EMPLOYEES COVERED?

Federal civilian employees hired before 1984 may not be covered. If you are this type of employee, but later switched to the "Federal Employee Retirement System," you will still be covered. In addition, even those federal employees who are not entitled to Social Security retirement benefits are still covered by the hospital insurance program.

Similarly, not all state and local government employees are covered. Originally, these employees were not part of Social Security coverage; however, the law has changed—if you are a government employee whose employer has entered a Section 218 agreement, you are covered. Check with your employer to find out whether this is the case.

Even if your employer does not have a Section 218 agreement with the Social Security Administration, you may still be covered. In July 1991, Congress passed a law extending coverage to state and local government employees, who are not otherwise covered, either by a Section 218 agreement or a public pension system.

All workers hired after 1986 have Medicare coverage even if they do not qualify for retirement benefits.

HOW SOCIAL SECURITY HAS EVOLVED OVER THE YEARS

Social Security was originally signed into law by Franklin D. Roosevelt (FDR) in 1935, a little over a year after creating a committee on Economic Security to try to find out what factors most influenced economic problems for ordinary people, and how the government could help them. FDR intended for this program to be "a cornerstone in a structure that is being built but is by no means complete" (SSA, 1984).

Initially, the program was meant to do two things:

- Assist current senior citizens by using government funds to pay pensions for the next 30 years.
- Allow younger people to provide for their own retirement pensions by requiring them to pay into the system (Miron & Weil, 1998).

During this initial period, all workers paid into the system via payroll taxes; however, people were not eligible for benefits unless they retired. No benefits were paid to anyone who made over $15 that month, regardless of their age. This requirement changed gradually, and, in 2000, Congress finally eliminated it altogether; today, anyone who meets the age threshold and has earned wages is eligible for Social Security retirement benefits.

In 1939, the Social Security Act was amended to include survivor and disability benefits. Farm workers and self-employed individuals didn't begin to receive benefits until 1950, a full 15 years after the program was first implemented, and it wasn't until 1972 that the Act was again amended to account for inflation and ensure that benefits would keep up with increases in the cost of living.

These changes to Social Security don't negate FDR's original vision for the program, which was based on European models. FDR understood that it was important for the government to provide assistance to seniors and that the program must be self-supporting. He also knew that the program he proposed was only the beginning of creating financial security for senior citizens and that the program would evolve over the years.

THE ROLE OF SOCIAL SECURITY IN RETIREMENT PLANNING

Social Security can—and should—play a role in your retirement planning. Despite the political back-and-forth about the program's solvency and longevity, it's mostly funded by taxes and won't run out of money any time soon. Thus, you should continue to track your Social Security earnings and consider how much you can expect to get per month.

Social Security carries benefits that other retirement plans don't, and that includes:

- You are guaranteed income; it doesn't matter what the economy is like or how the stock market is doing.
- Once you begin collecting Social Security, you will continue to receive payments for the rest of your life.
- Payments are adjusted to take inflation into account.
- Only 85% of your Social Security benefits are taxed, meaning you get to keep more of your money than you would with other retirement plans.

When creating your retirement plan, consider Social Security payments as a source of income. You can also calculate how much you will get based on which year you begin accepting benefits; although the minimum age is 62, you will receive a higher percentage of your earnings if you wait till 67 or 70 to begin collecting.

Before making any decisions, create a retirement budget. Consider the things you want to do after and during retirement, such as travel or spending on gifts for your grandchildren. How much will these things cost? What are your living expenses going to be? If you have a mortgage, will it be fully paid off before you retire, or do you need to ensure you have the money to pay it?

Take all these factors into account and list all your expenses. Then consider how much income you will need each month to not only meet your needs, but also live the way you want to. You can then check this against your Social Security estimated benefits (if you begin collecting at 62 or later). That will help you make a decision about when to start collecting as well as when to retire.

Your plan should include maximizing your Social Security benefits. Only 23% of people consider this factor (Vanguard, n.d.); be among them, so that you can get as much money as you're entitled to. After all, the more you can get from Social Security, the more income you'll have each month to pursue the things you dream of doing during your retirement.

It's important to be flexible, too. You may have dreamed of retiring at 65, but realize after doing your budget that you need to wait until the age of 70 to hit your financial goals. Similarly, you may have to change your mind about when you are planning to begin collecting Social Security benefits to maximize your earnings.

MEET THE FIRST SOCIAL SECURITY RECIPIENT

The first person to ever collect Social Security was named Ida May Fuller. She received her first retirement check only three years after the program was implemented in 1935, but she enjoyed her benefits for many years to come; she passed away at the age of 100 in 1975!

Ida May, whom friends affectionately dubbed "Aunt Ida," was born on September 6, 1874, on a small farm outside Ludlow, Vermont. She was a classmate of Calvin Coolidge, the 30th President of the United States! That wasn't the only brush she had with fame prior to becoming the first Social Security recipient; she also began working as a legal secretary in 1905, and her boss was none other than John C. Sargent, who later became Attorney General under Coolidge.

Like most Americans in 1939, Ida May wasn't sure what Social Security was all about or if it would really benefit her at all. She had gone into her local Social Security office to ask what this new program was all about, and the workers encouraged her to apply; nobody knew she'd be the first person to get a check from the new program. Ida May became a minor celebrity, and the Social Security Administration made a short film about her in 1950 in honor of the program's tenth anniversary (Whitelocks, 2015).

When she filled out her application, Ida May didn't expect to get anything back. Instead, she got $22.74 for her first month's payment, which is equivalent to about $500 in 2023 (CPI Calculator, 2023). She received almost $23,000 in payments over the course of her lifetime (Ring, 2015).

Ironically, Ida May was a staunch Republican from one of the only two states that didn't vote for FDR. While she admitted that Social Security helped pay all her expenses, shortly before her death in the 1970s, she stated that she believed it was wrong to increase benefit amounts and that doing so would hurt workers.

Nevertheless, the program clearly helped her enjoy her lengthy retirement; back in 1939, when it began, few people lived to be anywhere close to 100, but thanks to the lifetime payment provision of the program, she continued to enjoy a reasonable standard of living for the last 35 years of her life.

QUIZ YOURSELF!

Answer these "true or false" questions to see how much you've learned about Social Security.

- Social Security is paid for by the federal government.
- Social Security is only for retired people.
- My benefits are based on how much I've paid into the system.
- Social Security is intended to eliminate poverty among those who can't work, such as senior citizens and disabled people.

- Low-income workers receive very few Social Security benefits.
- FDR intended Social Security to be temporary, to help people during the Great Depression.
- Social Security does not adjust benefits to account for inflation.
- It's always best to claim your Social Security benefits as soon as you are eligible.
- The first recipient of Social Security was surprised that she received benefits.
- Social Security and Medicare are the same program.

SUMMARY

Social Security is an important part of retirement planning that is often misunderstood. Although originally conceived of as a pension program for senior citizens, nowadays it offers three programs: retirement benefits, survivor benefits, and disability benefits. Parents of disabled children may also receive benefits on their behalf. There are nine principles that govern Social Security; most importantly, it is a self-supporting program that is paid for by payroll taxes, and benefits are protected against inflation.

The purpose of this program is to protect against poverty by helping those who have retired or who cannot earn money to live more comfortably. The program was created in 1935, during the height of the Great Depression, as a new program to protect retirees, but has evolved into a larger program that now includes senior citizens who are still working, disabled people, and those who have been widowed.

It's important to understand how Social Security works and how to maximize your benefits so that you can plan appropriately for your retirement. Specifically, you should understand your benefit amounts and how they might change based on when you first begin collecting Social Security. You should also make a budget for retirement and figure out how Social Security payments fit into it.

Now that you know some of the history and purpose behind Social Security, and have a basic idea of how it works, you can begin learning how to maximize your benefits. The first step is to gain a solid understanding of who is eligible for benefits and what the exact criteria are for eligibility. We'll discuss that in the next chapter; turn the page when you're ready!

2

CLAIM WHAT'S YOURS - UNDERSTANDING ELIGIBILITY FOR SOCIAL SECURITY BENEFITS

Did you know that your benefits will be different depending on what program you apply for? Figuring out what you are eligible for, and how much you are entitled to, can be really confusing, but by the end of this chapter, you'll have a solid understanding of eligibility for retirement, disability, and survivor benefits.

As we discussed in the previous chapter, Social Security offers three separate programs:

- Retirement benefits for those over the age of 62
- Disability benefits for those who are unable to work due to a permanent health condition
- Survivor benefits for those who have lost a spouse

In some cases, children of beneficiaries may also be entitled to benefits. For example, often, parents of disabled children are able to collect benefits on their behalf until they turn 18, and in some cases, even after they reach adulthood.

EARNING CREDITS FOR RETIREMENT PAY

Although it's true that most people qualify for Social Security when they turn 62, age is not the only requirement for this benefit. Workers must be US citizens or legal permanent residents, and they must have earned 40 credits with the Social Security Administration.

Credits are determined using a formula; in general, workers can earn up to four credits per year and earn one credit for each $1,640 of covered income (AARP, 2022). In other words, if you earn, at least, $1,640 per quarter, you will earn a credit for that quarter toward your eligibility for Social Security.

To earn your four credits for the year, you must earn $6,560 per year ($1,640 x 4).

Don't let these numbers throw you off; if you're earning wages from a job, or receiving revenue from a business, you are likely getting your credits each year. Basically, you need to work for, at least, 10 years and make, at least, $6,560 each year to qualify for Social Security.

The exact amount you need to make to earn credits varies from year to year based on economic factors such as inflation. So, don't worry about the specific number; just remember that you need to have worked for, at least, 10 years to be eligible.

The number of credits you earn has no bearing on how much your monthly Social Security check will be. Your benefits are determined via a separate formula; we'll discuss how benefits are calculated later in this chapter. Credits are used solely to determine whether a worker is eligible for Social Security.

You can check your Social Security record online (at https://www.ssa.gov/myaccount/) to find out whether you have earned the appropriate number of credits to be eligible for retirement benefits and what your estimated benefits are likely to be, depending on when you start collecting.

TYPES OF BENEFITS

As we mentioned at the beginning of the chapter, there are different types of benefits, each with its own set of requirements.

- **Retirement benefits** are paid monthly to senior citizens. Seniors can begin to collect these benefits at any age past 62. The longer you wait to collect, the larger the benefit amount will be. Retirement benefits are not meant to be the retiree's only source of income, but many people depend on them to cover the costs of basic necessities. Benefit amounts are calculated based on your salary while you were working; benefits may also be available to spouses or ex-spouses even if they were homemakers and did not earn income.
- **Disability benefits** are available to those who can no longer work because of a disability or chronic health condition. Like retirement benefits, these are calculated based on your pre-disability salary. The amount of time you need to have worked to qualify for these benefits also varies. In some cases, spouses and divorced spouses are entitled to these benefits.

- **Supplemental security income** is available to disabled people who have never been able to work because of their disability, as well as some people who worked in the past but cannot work now due to some reason. The benefit amount depends on what other sources of income the person has and where they live.
- **Survivor benefits** are available to the spouse and children of someone who has passed away. The couple has to have been married at one point; divorced spouses may get benefits in some cases, but those who were never married are not eligible. Survivors who were married to a same-sex partner are eligible for the benefit as well. Benefits are calculated based on the worker's age at death, their salary, the survivors' ages, and their relationship to the person who has died.

Unused Social Security benefits are used to help pay others. If you don't claim the Social Security benefits that you are entitled to, those benefits are kept in trust and used to help pay other eligible people. You cannot get a refund of unused benefits, and if the person dies before they can collect, their family may also not be entitled to their unused retirement benefits.

TAXES AND SOCIAL SECURITY

If a person earns more than $25,000 in a given year ($32,000 for married couples filing jointly), they must pay federal tax on their Social Security benefits.

In addition, 12 states currently levy taxes against Social Security benefits:

- Colorado
- Connecticut
- Kansas
- Minnesota
- Missouri
- Montana
- Nebraska
- New Mexico
- Rhode Island
- Utah
- Vermont
- West Virginia

If you do not live in one of these states, you do not have to pay state taxes on your benefits.

HOW MUCH DO WIDOWS GET?

Survivor benefits are usually 100% of the primary benefit amount the deceased would have received if they were still alive. If a former spouse was married to the person who passed away for, at least, 10 years and has not remarried, they are also entitled to this amount.

SOCIAL SECURITY BENEFITS ARE RECALCULATED YEARLY

Every year, the SSA recalculates your benefits. Benefit amounts can change based on inflation or other economic factors. In addition, if you are below full retirement age and receiving benefits, the amount can be offset by wages or earnings from self-employment. However, passive income, such as investment income, does not affect your benefit amount.

HOW RETIREMENT BENEFITS ARE CALCULATED

Your retirement benefits are calculated on how much you earned while you were working. Many people change jobs, start a new business, or go through periods of low income after being laid off, so your income might not have been steady over the course of your adult life. For this reason, Social Security benefits are calculated based on an average of the 35 highest-earning years of your life. This average is then adjusted to account for inflation so that you won't be penalized if your highest-earning years were a long time ago when wages and prices were both lower than they are today. After this adjustment, the SSA applies a formula to determine how much money you are entitled to receive each month.

You can begin taking Social Security at the age of 62, but if you do, you will receive 30% less each month than you would if you waited until you reached full retirement age (i.e., 66 or 67 in 2023, depending on when you were born). Conversely, if you wait until you are 70, you will receive about 132% more than you would if you took your benefits earlier! This benefit reduction is permanent; your Social Security benefits won't increase when you hit 67 if you take it at 62. However, the SSA will continue to apply cost-of-living increases to your benefit amounts each year even if you take it early. If you continue working while taking Social Security benefits before you reach the age of 67, your benefits will be reduced by $1 for every $2 you earn.

In addition, if you wait until you reach the full retirement age, you will not lose any benefits if you continue to work after you file your first claim.

WORKING WHILE ON DISABILITY

The SSA encourages individuals to work while going through the process of applying for disability. This allows the SSA to see the full extent of your disability and determine how capable you are of maintaining full-time employment (SAMSHA, n.d.)

After you are approved for disability benefits, working might affect those benefits in different ways, depending on the type of disability benefit you are receiving.

Supplemental Security Income, or SSI, is meant for people who are unable to earn significant income because of a disability. The disability can be physical, mental, or both. The SSA excludes certain income from its calculation of benefits:

- The first $20 of income is excluded, whether or not that income is earned from a job.
- The first $65 of income from a job is also excluded.
- Money saved toward an educational or vocational goal, as outlined in the recipient's "Plan to Achieve Self-Support" (PASS), does not count against SSI benefits.
- Students may be allowed an exemption of a certain amount of income if they are under the age of 22 and go to school full-time.
- Impairment-related costs to get to work are subtracted from income. For example, if the person needs to hire a transportation service for people with their disability, or needs special medication to be able to perform their job, these costs would be excluded.

After calculating these amounts, the SSA then divides the remaining income amount in half and pays benefits based on this amount.

For example, suppose a person earns $750 from a part-time job. The SSA would then calculate as follows:

- Subtract $20 of generally excluded income.
- Subtract $65 of job-related income.
- Subtract $150 in savings for an educational goal.
- Subtract $100 in impairment-related costs.
- Total exclusions are $335.
- Subtract this from total income to get countable income of $365.
- Divide $365 in half to get $182.50.
- Subtract $182.50 from the maximum benefit amount to get the amount of benefits the person is entitled to.

Social Security Disability Insurance (SSDI) is calculated a bit differently. Benefits are based on past earnings, and a person who is on SSDI is allowed to work for nine months out of a rolling five-year period without penalty to see if they are capable of holding down a job. This means that if you work a full nine months, after that, you will see a reduction to your benefits; however, you can divide those nine months over five years. For example, suppose you got SSDI benefits beginning in 2023, and that summer, you tried working but quit after a month because it was too stressful. If you try again and work three months in 2024 before quitting, you still have another five months you can work any time between 2024 and 2028. After five years, your trial period starts again, so if you don't return to work until 2029, those four months of your trial no longer count.

If you complete your trial period, you still have a three-year extended eligibility period. This means that if you don't earn over a certain amount during a given month, you will still receive your full check during that month.

As with SSI, SSDI recipients can subtract impairment-related work expenses and money saved toward their educational or vocational goal on their "PASS plan" from their total income. If their countable income falls below the threshold, they can still receive their full check.

People with disability may continue to be eligible for Medicaid or Medicare benefits, depending on their income level. If they become disqualified from medical or cash benefits because of their income level, and then are again unable to work within five years, their reinstatement application will be expedited.

OTHER CONSIDERATIONS

If you are working while on Social Security and you are laid off, you can continue to get your Social Security checks while taking unemployment. Keep in mind that while you can collect both, your Social Security income might impact the amount of unemployment income you are entitled to.

However, you cannot receive both retirement and disability benefits at the same time. However, when you reach the age of 65, your disability benefits will automatically be converted to retirement benefits. The amount you receive will not change; the only difference is the program under which you will receive your money.

Keep in mind that if you make over $25,000/year, whether or not you are working, you will have to pay federal taxes on your Social Security benefits.

CHECK YOUR UNDERSTANDING

Check your understanding of eligibility for Social Security with this brief "true or false" quiz.

- All three Social Security programs (Retirement, Disability, and Survivor) pay the same number of benefits.
- You need to have worked for, at least, 10 years to be eligible for Social Security.
- The more credits you have, the larger the retirement benefit you will receive.
- You do not have to be a US citizen to receive benefits.
- If you are divorced, your ex-spouse might be eligible for Social Security benefits based on your earnings.
- If you work after taking retirement benefits, you will lose part of your benefits no matter how old you are.
- There are two different disability benefit programs.
- You cannot work at all while on SSI or SSDI, or you will lose your benefits.
- Social Security income is never taxable.
- You are ineligible for unemployment benefits if you receive retirement benefits.

SUMMARY

Understanding different Social Security programs, and whether you are eligible for them is crucial to being able to maximize your benefits. In this chapter, we discussed the various Social Security programs and how benefits are calculated for each one of them.

While many people think Social Security and retirement benefits are synonymous, this is only one of three programs that the SSA offers. In addition to retirement benefits, the SSA is responsible for both disability and survivor benefits. Disability benefits are for people who cannot work full-time due to an injury, illness, or condition, while survivor benefits are for people who have lost a spouse to death. To qualify for retirement benefits, three things must be true: you must be over the age of 62; earned, at least, 40 credits through paying payroll taxes; and be either a US citizen or a legal permanent resident.

Credits are earned automatically as you are working. Workers earn up to four credits a year by paying payroll taxes; as of 2023, they must earn $6,560/year to earn these four credits. Workers must earn 40 credits to qualify for retirement benefits, which means they have to work for, at least, 10 years. Credits are not used to calculate your benefit amount; they are only used for eligibility purposes.

Retirement benefits are calculated based on your average income, which is then corrected to account for inflation. The average is taken using the 35 years when you earned the highest income. If you did not work for 35 consecutive years, any year where you were unemployed is given a value of zero dollars.

Although you can begin getting Social Security at the age of 62, you will receive fewer benefits if you take it then. In addition, your benefits will be reduced by $1 for every $2 you earn if you continue to work while collecting benefits. Your benefit amount will not increase when you reach the age of 65 in this scenario; however, after 65, you will no longer lose any benefits if you continue working. If you delay receiving benefits until you are past retirement age, you will get an 8% increase for each year of delay, which means that if you delay until the age of 70, you will receive 132% of the benefits you are entitled to. Retirement benefits are taxable at the federal level if you make over $25,000/year (or $32,000, if you are part of a married couple that files joint tax returns).

If you are receiving disability benefits, the SSA may do a complex series of calculations to figure out your benefit amount. Benefits vary based on whether you are on SSI, SSDI, or both, and each program has rules about how "money earned from working while on disability" affects a recipient's benefits. In order to encourage people with disabilities to work, the SSA offers trial periods in which you can work without penalty for a short period of time. Currently, you can work for nine months over a five-year period without losing any of your SSDI benefits. In addition, you can continue to receive SSDI for three years after beginning a new job, if your income doesn't meet a certain threshold.

You can receive unemployment and retirement benefits at the same time, but you can't receive retirement and disability benefits simultaneously. If you receive disability benefits, they will be converted to retirement benefits when you turn 65, but the amount you receive will not change.

Now that you understand the various Social Security programs and their eligibility requirements, the next step is to learn how to maximize your benefits. Many people don't know how to do this and end up with less money than they are entitled to. But this doesn't have to be you! In the next chapter, we will begin discussing strategies for how to maximize your benefits.

Turn the page when you are ready to get started!

3

REAPING REWARDS - HOW TO OPTIMIZE YOUR SOCIAL SECURITY BENEFITS

Getting the maximum benefit amount isn't as easy as filling out your Social Security claim forms. There are many options you have to consider if you want to get as much money as possible each month.

In addition to making sure you are applying to the best program for your needs, you'll need to think about things like whether you should claim your benefits right now or wait a few years. If you are not at full retirement age, you'll also need to decide when to retire.

These are monumental decisions, not only because retirement changes your life but also because your approach to Social Security affects your financial future. If you claim benefits just because you can, without thinking things through, you may leave money on the table that you would need to pursue the life of your dreams.

Optimizing your Social Security benefits requires strategic thinking. In the last chapter, we went over what the different programs are, and gave you a sneak preview of the decisions you may need to make if you want to get as much money as possible. Now, we'll begin talking about strategy. By the end of this chapter, you'll have a solid understanding of different strategies for optimizing your Social Security benefits and a better idea of what plan will best meet your needs.

TIMING IS EVERYTHING: WHAT TO CONSIDER WHEN CLAIMING RETIREMENT BENEFITS

If you want to maximize your retirement benefits, you should consider how long you can afford to wait before you file your first claim.

As of 2023, you can begin getting retirement benefits at the age of 62, but it's not always the best idea. The SSA doesn't consider you fully retired until age 67 (as of 2023), so if you take benefits earlier than that, you won't get as much money each month and your benefits won't increase once you hit 67. In addition, any wages you receive from work will count against your Social Security retirement benefit if you are between the ages of 62 and 67. Once you hit 67, that is no longer an issue, but you'll lose money each month in the meantime.

Economic research suggests that almost everyone who is currently aged 45 to 62 would benefit from waiting until they are, at least, 67 to begin receiving retirement benefits and that 90% of this age group are best off waiting until they are 70 (Altig et al, 2022). However, only 10% of people wait that long, which means that a majority of Americans are leaving money on their table. The median loss for Americans, thanks to them not following this advice, is $182,370 (Konish, 2023). This means that half the people who claim too early lose MORE than this!

There are three reasons why waiting might be the best option for you:

- **You might have the opportunity to increase your total benefits:** Social Security benefits are calculated on the 35 highest-paid years of income. So, if you work an extra few years, you might earn more money during those years and thus your benefits will be calculated based on that income.
- **You avoid reduced payments if you wait until you are at least 67:** As mentioned earlier, you will receive fewer benefits if you begin collecting retirement checks before you reach full retirement age—the SSA reduces your monthly benefits by 30% and that reduction is permanent rather than changing when you turn 67. For example, you might receive $2,000/month if you wait until the age of 67, but only $1,400/month if you begin collecting at the age of 62.
- **Delayed retirement to beyond age 67 adds to your benefits:** You will receive an 8 percent increase in benefits for each year you delay between 67 and 70. So, if you wait until you are 70 to begin collecting retirement benefits, you will get a vastly higher sum each month than if you collected earlier.

Thus, in most cases, it makes sense to delay collecting retirement benefits. Ironically, this is especially true for lower-income people, who may be more dependent on their monthly benefit check to meet their needs, and who also may be more tempted to collect earlier so that they can have an additional source of income before they fully retire.

If Social Security is not the only retirement plan you have, it's easier to delay your claim. For example, if you have a 401k or other retirement savings account, you might be able to withdraw funds from that account to help with your monthly expenses until you cross the age threshold of 67. However, you should be aware that these types of accounts make money by investing your savings in the stock market, so how much money is in store for you depends on how well the economy is doing and whether your money has been invested wisely. Conversely, your retirement benefit will be the same amount of money each month, and there is no risk that you will lose a part of your benefits if the stock market crashes.

While waiting until 67, or even 70, makes sense for the majority of people, there is one situation where you may want to collect earlier: if you have a terminal illness and don't expect to survive until the age of 70. Your retirement benefits are not transferable to anyone else, so you'll lose that money if you don't collect. However, in this case, you may want to look into how survivor benefits (discussed later in this chapter) work in addition to claiming your retirement benefits, so that you can make sure your heirs are taken care of.

HOW TO DECIDE WHAT'S RIGHT FOR YOU

If it's best for almost everyone to wait until they are 70 years old to start collecting their Social Security benefits, then why don't most people do it?

Some people may not be aware that there's any difference in benefits, but others may feel they can't afford to delay. If you are struggling financially, claiming your Social Security benefits early might seem like the best solution, especially if you don't have other sources of retirement income.

That's why it's best to have a comprehensive retirement plan in place long before you turn 62. But whether you do or not, you should do some analysis to determine what's the best time for you to begin collecting your retirement benefits.

It's helpful to calculate how much your monthly payment will change based on when you begin collecting your benefits. You can check your estimated benefit amounts online by signing into your SSA account. This will tell you what your lifetime earnings are so far, and what your estimated monthly benefit amount will be if you start collecting at various ages. You can also put your numbers into the SSA's online retirement calculator to get a rough idea of how your benefits will change, depending on when you claim them.

REASONS PEOPLE DON'T WAIT TO FILE

Although you can maximize your benefits by delaying your claim past the age of 70, there are several reasons people don't do it:

- **They don't expect to live that long:** If you have a terminal illness, you might only have a few months or years left. In this case, you may not see much, or any, of your money if you wait.
- **They have cash flow issues:** If you are struggling to pay your monthly bills, it can be hard, or even impossible, to wait. A guaranteed $1000 or more per month may seem like the best option for keeping the lights on and enough food on your table.

- **They don't care about maximizing their benefits:** Some people may want to live a full, active life, and it's easier to do that if you grab whatever money is available to you NOW than if you wait. Or, if you're stuck at a job that makes you miserable, and taking your retirement benefit now will allow you to escape it and have some fun during your remaining years, you might decide to take a smaller monthly check in exchange for not having to force yourself to work.

- **The math shows it won't make much of a difference:** If you live for long enough, you'll receive the same total benefits whether you start early or late. If you have an unusually long-life expectancy, you might decide to take your retirement benefits early so that you have some money coming in, with the understanding that, eventually, you will have received the same amount that you would if you wait.

- **They have a special situation:** Some people may be on disability or be entitled to survivor benefits. However, their retirement benefit might be greater than these other benefits. In this case, it makes sense to take retirement earlier.

The bottom line is that everyone's situation is different, so you should consider all the factors before deciding when to take your benefits. Although you will maximize the amount you get per month if you wait until age 70 to start collecting, it may be to your overall advantage to begin collecting earlier.

To determine what is best for you, you can do a "break-even analysis." This involves calculating how old you will be when you will receive roughly the same amount, no matter when you begin collecting (Fontinelle, 2023). For example, suppose you get $1,500/month if you start at age 62, or $2,000/month if you start at age 66. At age 78, you will have received $288,000 regardless of whether you take benefits early ($1,500/month x 12 months/one year x 16 years) or delay until age 66 ($2000/month x 12 months/one year x 12 years). Thus, the earlier you claim benefits, the longer you have to live to reach your break-even age. So, if you expect to live into your 80s, it makes sense to wait until you are 66 or older to begin collecting benefits. However, if you don't expect to live that long, you won't get much benefit from waiting and might want to claim your benefits earlier.

DOING A BENEFIT-COST RATIO TO HELP YOU DECIDE

To determine whether it's worth it to claim your retirement benefits early versus claiming other types of benefits, you can do a "benefit-cost ratio," or BCR. This analysis tells you whether the benefits of doing so are worth the cost.

To do a BCR, divide the total cash benefits by the cost. If the result of this calculation is greater than 1.0, it means you will profit from claiming your benefits now. If it is less than 1.0, you will lose money if you do this instead of delaying your claim.

For example, suppose that if you claim your retirement benefits at the age of 62 (Option A), you will receive $700/month, while you will get $1,000/month if you wait until you are 67 (Option B). Consider your life expectancy to calculate your total benefits for each option. For this example, let's say you expect to live to about age 85. You will also want to calculate your total expenses per year so you can see how much money you will actually keep each month.

First, multiply each monthly amount by 12 to get a yearly amount. That's $8400/year under Option A and $12,000/year under Option B. However, you will also need to subtract your expenses per year. Let's say your average expenses are $8,000 per year. So, you are getting to keep $400/year under Option A and $4,000 a year under Option B.

Next, multiply that by the number of years you expect to live. Under Option A, that's 23 years (85-62), while under Option B that's 18 years (85-67). So, your total benefit amounts would be:

- Option A: $9,200
- Option B: $92,000

Now, to get your BCR, you would need to know your total costs and total benefits. Subtract your Option A amount from your Option B amount to get the costs of choosing Option A. This number is $82,800. Let's plug that into the formula:

Total. benefits/Total costs = $9,200/82,800 = 0.111

This number is less than 1.0, so it is not profitable to choose this option. Note, that if you forget to consider your yearly expenses and merely look at the benefit amounts, you'd be looking at:

- Option A: $193,200
- Option B: $216,000
- Cost: $22,800

CBR: $193,200/$22,800 = 8.47, which would appear to be quite profitable despite the loss of income. Thus, it is important to consider profit, and not just income, when making this calculation.

CONSIDERING WHEN TO RETIRE

Deciding when to take your retirement benefits may also depend on when you choose to retire. More and more people are considering retiring before the age of 65—you may need your Social Security check at 62, if you do so.

There are several pros and cons to early retirement that you should consider before making the leap:

+ Pros

- It may be better for your mental and physical health if you can leave a draining job earlier.
- You'll have more time to spend with loved ones or doing activities that you enjoy.
- You may be able to travel (if you can afford it).
- You might be able to change careers or start a new business.

— Cons

For some people, retiring early can lead to mental and physical health problems, especially if they are already at risk.

- It can cause extra financial stress.
- You'll get fewer benefits per month if you claim Social Security early.
- Retirement savings will have to last longer.
- You may need to find health insurance.
- You might become bored, feel purposeless, or miss your old job.

One of the biggest concerns is the financial impact of retiring early. Suppose you earn $36,000/year. In that case, your job brings you a little less than $3,000/month when you factor in taxes.

If you're 62 years old, you can retire and take Social Security benefits at about $900/month—about a third of what you made before retirement. You'll likely have to supplement this with other retirement income or income from a second job (although if you take a new job, your benefits will decrease). And retirement accounts are dependent on the stock market, so if the economy crashes, you could lose money in your 401k or IRA. All of this adds up to financial stress, so it may be best to remain on the job.

On the other hand, suppose you're making over $100,000 and are bringing in $8,000/month. Here, your Social Security benefit would be even more significantly reduced—$1,685/month! But you may have more money in savings or fewer expenses because you earn more, so it may be manageable. If so, retiring early and taking less income might be a suitable trade-off for not having to work.

Of course, this decision is also dependent on other factors such as what your expenses are, who else you are supporting financially, and what kind of retirement package your company offers you. A person who is helping support small grandchildren or whose spouse doesn't work is in a different financial situation than someone who has no dependents. The existence of other pensions and how much money you have in savings will also impact your decision.

If early retirement isn't financially feasible, there are a few other options you might consider. In the post-COVID world, working remotely from home has become fairly common. If your company will allow you to do so, consider working remotely, at least, a few days a week. This will help cut out some stressors associated with work, such as dealing with traffic on your commute or having to spend time with difficult coworkers.

Another option might be to cut back on your hours. Some jobs will allow older workers to become semi-retired by adjusting schedules, so that they only work two or three days a week. This may mean a partial loss of income, but if it's significantly more than what you would get if you take retirement benefits, it may be a reasonable compromise.

Finally, if you have vacation days accrued, use them! If one of the reasons you want to retire early is so that you can travel, taking a vacation might work just as well, especially since you're getting paid for it.

CONSIDERATIONS IF YOU ARE MARRIED

Married couples need to consider the impact on their spouse's benefits of various options for claiming Social Security retirement checks, which won't be a factor if you aren't married—of course, if you're widowed, or have children or grandchildren you are financially responsible for, you still have other considerations even if you don't have a partner. If you're married, you might want to consider:

- **The age of your spouse and the difference between your ages:** If your spouse is not yet retirement age and won't reach it until long after you do, any decision you make will impact their eventual spousal benefits. If your spouse is older than you, you'll want to consider your options carefully; you may want to hold off as long as possible and claim their benefit in the event that they pass away first.

- **Whether your spouse is also working:** If only one partner is working, then the other may be entitled to spousal benefits. This will impact your bottom line more than if both partners are working and entitled to their own benefits.

- **Whether there are significant differences between the amount of money each of you are entitled to:** For married couples, either spouse claiming early could impact both of their benefits. If one spouse is entitled to more benefits, that spouse may want to hold off so that they can maximize their benefit. In addition, if one spouse dies, the other is entitled to whichever benefit is bigger— their own or their partner's. So, if you have the bigger benefit you might want to refrain from claiming it right now, so that your spouse can take it in the event you die first.

- **Whether either of you is subject to special rules such as the Windfall Elimination Provision or the Government Pension Offset:** If either of you is, that'll lower your total benefit amount, so you need to know this before making any decisions.

- **Whether you need cash right now:** The biggest concern for most couples is cash flow. If you're having trouble paying your bills, saving, or affording certain things, it doesn't help you to know that you'll get a large benefit five to eight years from now.

- **What your life expectancies are:** If either of you doubts that you will not live to be 80, then you may want to consider taking your retirement benefits earlier so you can live comfortably for the remainder of your life.

- **What your work plans are:** If you plan to keep working, or your spouse does, that will put you in a different financial situation than if either one of you is dead-set on retiring in the next few years.

- **Former relationships:** If either of you is a widow, or is divorced from someone who is still alive, that will also affect your benefits. Widowed spouses may be entitled to survivor benefits, which might be bigger than what you could get if you took your retirement benefit right now. And if you are divorced, your ex-spouse might be entitled to spousal benefits if you were married for 10 years or longer.

- **Do you have any unmarried children under the age of 19?** If you are legally or morally obligated to take care of children, that is going to impact your bottom line, and you need to think carefully about whether it makes financial sense to take retirement benefits right now.

HOW YOUR SPOUSE CLAIMING BENEFITS MAY IMPACT YOUR DECISION

Both current and divorced spouses can, in some cases, claim your retirement benefits based on your work history rather than their own. This is called a "spousal benefit."

If your spouse doesn't qualify for their own retirement benefits—for example, if they stayed at home with children rather than working outside the home, then they are entitled to spousal benefits. If they take this benefit before the age of 67, they will only be entitled to half of what they will get if they wait. Spouses do not get delayed retirement benefits, so there is no advantage to them waiting beyond the age of 67. However, if you are in a position to be able to work at a high-paying job until you are 70, you will increase your total benefit amount, which means that your spouse will get a bigger benefit, too, if you both wait until then to begin claiming benefits.

You have several strategies to consider, so here's how to begin to make this decision.

The best way to begin is to get both of your estimated benefits from your Social Security Administration accounts. That way, you have an idea of how much money each of you will be entitled to, if you claim benefits at various ages. Knowing these numbers can help you see what will be financially best for you. When comparing your estimates, pay special attention to which one is higher. That person has higher earnings, and the gap between your earnings and your spouse's will help you decide which strategy to use.

Many couples use a "split strategy"—the person who earns more delays claiming Social Security benefits, while the person who earns less claims them as soon as possible. This can help maximize the amount of money coming in because the higher earner will receive greater benefits when they finally make their claim, but the lower earner will have been getting retirement benefits for a while by the time that happens.

For example, suppose Mark is entitled to $700/month if he collects at age 62, $1000/month if he collects at age 67, or $1,320/month if he collects at age 70. Conversely, Mark's partner, Sally, is entitled to $1,050/month if she collects at age 62, $1,500/month if she collects at age 67, and $1,980/month if she collects at age 70. Using a split strategy, Mark takes the $700/month, while Sally waits until she's entitled to the full $1,980. By the time Sally is ready to collect eight years later, Mark has already collected $67,200 in benefits, which has greatly helped them afford the life they wanted to lead.

If one couple earns more than twice the other, both spouses may want to eventually claim benefits on the same record. To do this, the lower-earning partner would claim their own benefits early, as described above, and then file a claim for spousal benefits when their partner begins collecting benefits.

BENEFITS FOR DIVORCED SPOUSES

The basic rule for divorced spouses is that if you were married for 10 years or longer, and have not remarried, you can claim half of your ex-partner's benefits. This doesn't mean that your ex-partner gets only half of their benefit; they will still get the full amount, while you just get half that amount.

Using the same example as above, if Mark and Sally were married for 10 years before their divorce, and Mark has not remarried, he is entitled to a benefit of half of that $1,980/month that we calculated Sally was entitled to in the previous section. This comes out to $990/month. Sally would still get the full $1,980/month, and if she remarried, Mark's claim would not affect her new spouse's benefits either.

It's important to check both your own and your ex-partner's record if you're considering claiming divorced spousal benefits. That way, you can check how much you would get against what you are entitled to if you make a claim on your own record. If you have your ex's Social Security number, you can check this online. If you don't have that information, the Social Security Administration can look up the record for you; you'll need your ex's full name, date and place of birth, and the name of their parents.

You can still apply for divorced spouse benefits without your ex's Social Security number; you only need that to look up the earnings record online. Spousal benefits don't increase if you wait past full retirement age, so you can apply for them at the age of 67. You can still file a claim even if your ex-spouse hasn't begun collecting yet (if you've been divorced for two years).

SURVIVOR BENEFITS AND STRATEGIES FOR WIDOWS

If a post-retirement-age spouse passes away, the surviving spouse is entitled to the larger of their own benefit or their late spouse's benefit. So, if you earn more money than your partner, it might be best to delay making your claim. This way, if you pass away first, your spouse will get a larger check. It's heartbreaking to lose a spouse, so it may be difficult to think about your options if you are a new widow or widower. But there are some important financial decisions you will need to make.

Let's look at the example of Kathy, a recent widow.

Kathy's husband, Bill, passed away recently. Kathy is 66 years old and in good health, and she's considering her options. Bill was already collecting retirement benefits at the time of his death, and those benefits were $300/month (more than what Kathy is entitled to). However, Kathy would like to retire if possible, so that she can move closer to her children now that Bill is gone—but she won't reach retirement age for another year, so if she takes her retirement benefits now, they'll be reduced by 30%.

When it comes to retirement benefits, Kathy has the same options as everyone else:

- Take early retirement, which means her benefits will be reduced by 30%
- Wait a year and receive 100% of her benefit

- Wait until she's 70 and receive 132% of her benefit

As a widow, Kathy also has an additional option. She can file for survivor benefits. Survivor benefits would allow her to receive income based on Bill's earnings. However, when she later files for her own retirement benefits, that would be calculated on her own earnings, not Bill's. Thus, if she wants, she can file for survivor benefits now and full retirement benefits when she is 70. Conversely, she can take an early retirement benefit, and then apply for survivor benefits next year when she turns 67. She'll need to run the numbers to see which strategy is better for her long-term.

Let's say Kathy's delayed retirement benefit would be $2,640/month, and her early retirement benefit would be $1400/month. Her survivor benefit now would be 99% of Bill's retirement benefit, so if Bill was entitled to $1,500/month, her survivor benefit would be $1,485/month. If she waits a year, she will get the full $1,500. In this case, it makes sense for Kathy to take the survivor benefit right now and wait until she turns 70 to take her retirement benefit. This will allow her to get a little bit more now than she would if she took retirement benefits now, and a lot more once she files for retirement.

Survivor benefits are available to widows of any age who are taking care of children under the age of 16 (if your child is permanently disabled, you may be able to get these benefits even if they are adults). Widows without children can receive reduced survivor benefits starting at age 60—this benefit is 71%-99% of your late spouse's retirement benefit, while those with young or permanently disabled children receive 75% of their spouse's retirement benefit regardless of their children's age.

THE EARNINGS TEST FOR SSA BENEFITS

Whether you take survivor benefits or worker benefits, keep the "Earnings Test" in mind. The SSA has rules for how much you can earn via wages if you take early retirement benefits. In 2023, workers under the age of 67 may not earn more than $21,240. However, if you are 66, and going on 67 the year you apply, the limit changes to $56,520. These limits are set by the SSA and may be subject to changes every year depending on the economy.

If you earn more than this maximum amount while taking retirement benefits, the SSA will take $1 away from your total benefit for every $2 earned. Remember, this only applies if you are under the age of 67. For example, Kathy is turning 67 this year, so if she earns $60,000 this year, she will exceed the earnings limit by $3,480. Thus, her annual benefit will be reduced by half of that excess, or $1,740 (to be precise). For example, if she has an annual benefit of $20,000/year, and earns more than $60,000 this year, her annual benefit this year will be $18,260 ($20,000 - $1,740). Benefits are paid monthly, so that would come out to $1,521.67/month. Conversely, if she didn't earn more than $56,520 this year, she would get the full benefit of $20,000 per year, which comes out to $1,666.67 per month.

QUIZ YOURSELF!

Read these three scenarios and list the pros and cons of taking Social Security early for each one. Then decide what the worker's best strategy is.

Scenario 1

Jennifer has just enough money coming in from her job to pay her bills, but doesn't have anything left over to save or spend. She just turned 62 and plans to keep working, but she would like to put more money in her pocket, so she's considering claiming early retirement. She also has a 401k from her job, but thanks to a recent economic crash, it has lost money. Should Jennifer take her retirement benefits now?

Our answer: It is best for Jennifer to take her benefits now. Her benefits will be reduced slightly by her wages and she will receive less of a benefit than she would if she waited, but it's the best way to reduce her financial pressure.

Scenario 2

Marilla and Matthew are both still going strong at the ages of 62 and 64, respectively, and have recently adopted their two grand-children after the tragic death of the children's mother. Marilla makes more money than Matthew because of her side business of selling plum puffs at a local farmer's market, but now that they have two children to take care of, she's wondering if it might be a good idea for one or both of them to take their retirement benefits early to pay for extra expenses related to child care. What should be their best strategy?

Our answer: Matthew should take his retirement benefits now, while Marilla continues working and waits to take her benefit. That way, the couple has money coming in to help them with the children. Another strategy could be, if Marilla and Matthew were dependent upon their daughter, to consider whether they qualify for survivor benefits.

Scenario 3

Gary was looking forward to spending his golden years traveling and doing all the things he never got to do, but he recently learned his cancer metastasized into his lungs. He is likely going to die within the next few years. Gary is 64 this year and feels like his life has been unfairly cut short. Should he take his retirement benefits now?

Our answer: Yes, Gary may not live to see 70, so there is little point in him delaying taking his benefit., assuming he's unmarried.

SUMMARY

In this information-packed chapter, we discussed all the factors that go into maximizing your Social Security retirement benefits.

One of the biggest questions people have pertains to what age they should start taking benefits. While you are allowed to begin collecting retirement benefits at 62, there are some disadvantages: you'll receive a permanent reduction of 30% which means getting smaller checks each month. Conversely, if you wait until you're 70, you'll get 132% of your full benefit amount. For most people, waiting makes the most sense, but if you're strapped for cash or are facing a terminal diagnosis, it might make more sense to take your benefits as early as possible.

If you are married, divorced, or widowed, the decision becomes more complex. Taking benefits early could affect any survivor or spousal benefit your partner files in the future, and if you are divorced, you may be entitled to spousal or survivor benefits if you have not remarried. Similarly, widows are entitled to survivor benefits; they may also be entitled to these if their ex-spouse passes away, but in this case, the widow must not remarry before the age of 60 to qualify for these benefits.

Finally, if you are disabled, you have to decide when to file for disability benefits, and when to file for retirement benefits, as you can't take both at once.

Now that you've learned all of this information, don't get over-whelmed! Think about what is best for your situation and start putting a plan into action. Once you have a good grip on your Social Security retirement plan, you'll need to know how to cover health care costs after you retire. In the next chapter, we'll go over some basics related to Medicare.

Turn the page when you're ready to start learning about it!

4

BEYOND THE BASICS - SPECIAL CASES IN SOCIAL SECURITY

It's a waste of time to be angry about my disability. One has to get on with life and I haven't done badly.

— STEPHEN HAWKING

Social Security offers unique provisions for those who are dealing with disability, either their own or their child's. Having a physical or mental disability can make certain aspects of your life more challenging than they are for non-disabled people. Some of those challenges involve expensive finances—therapies, interventions, or special educational programs, and disabled adults may be limited in their ability to work, making it harder for them to earn the income needed to provide for these special services.

That's why Social Security offers disability payments for those who are taking care of themselves or disabled children. In this chapter, we will explore all the options available so that you can maximize your benefits if you are dealing with any such special circumstances.

BENEFITS FOR DISABLED ADULT CHILDREN

Both minors and adults with disabilities may be eligible for benefits under the Social Security disability program. If you are caring for a disabled adult child, there are certain things you should know about the benefits entitled to you on your child's behalf.

There are two different programs:

- Minors with disabilities, as well as some disabled adult children, may qualify for Social Supplemental Income (SSI), which is a program meant for people who cannot work due to a disability.
- Disabled adults, including some who have been disabled since childhood, may be eligible for Social Security Disability Insurance (SSDI). This program is considered a "child's benefit" because it is paid against the parent's Social Security earnings record; SSDI is available for adults who developed a disability prior to the age of 22.

In order to receive SSDI, the applicant must meet the Social Security Administration's criteria for disability and must be unmarried. If your child is already receiving SSI payments, don't assume that also they don't qualify for SSDI. Check the eligibility criteria and apply on their behalf if they appear to be eligible. In addition, if your child's circumstances have changed since their 18th birthday, they may be eligible for higher benefits than before. For example, if a parent has passed away or is now retired, that can also affect eligibility and benefit amounts. Thus, it's important to talk to an advocate at the Social Security Administration about your situation to find out what your child may be entitled to. Once a disabled adult child has been approved for disability payments, the payments will continue for life, as long as the adult child remains disabled.

BENEFITS FOR DISABLED MINORS

You may qualify for SSI benefits on behalf of your disabled minor (child under the age of 18), depending on your household income. The child must have a medical condition that makes them disabled for, at least, 12 months or is expected to result in their death. This benefit is called the "Child Disability Benefit Program."

In order to receive these benefits, you must go through a rigorous application process. The process involves sharing detailed information and documentation about your child's medical condition and how it affects their daily functioning. You will have to sign releases for therapists, doctors, and teachers to provide your child's private health information as part of the application. In some cases, the SSA will need additional information and require their own medical examination of your child. The SSA will pay for the exam and provide the doctor if this is the case.

It usually takes about three to six months for the SSA to make a decision. However, if your child has a serious physical disability such as muscular dystrophy, total blindness, or cerebral palsy, the SSA may make payments while they are processing your application. You will not have to pay this back if the SSA ultimately decides your child does not qualify for SSI.

Children do not qualify for SSDI payments until they reach the age of 18.

THE PICKLE AMENDMENT

The Pickle Amendment, introduced in 1976, will help ensure that your disabled children remain eligible for Medicaid while receiving SSI or SSDI.

This amendment is named after former Representative James Pickle, who was worried that the annual cost-of-living increase in Social Security benefits would push some SSI recipients over the maximum income allowed to remain eligible for benefits. This unfair situation would cause some people to have to choose between SSI and Medicaid—and if they needed medical treatment to manage their disability, and SSI to meet their basic living expenses, this would become an impossible decision.

Thus, the Pickle Amendment changed the Medicaid eligibility rules so that cost-of-living increases are not counted toward income for the purpose of determining Medicaid eligibility. This means that if you or your child receives SSI or SSDI, the annual increase in your benefits to cover changes in cost of living will not count when Medicaid examines your eligibility.

DECEASED PARENT BENEFITS

As we discussed in Chapter 3, adults may be entitled to survivor benefits when their partner dies. In addition, children may be eligible for these benefits if a parent dies.

- Children under 18 are entitled to benefits if:
- A parent is collecting retirement benefits or disability benefits at the time of their death.

A parent passes away who has paid enough into Social Security to be entitled to benefits when they retire.

Children can receive these benefits if they are unmarried and under the age of 18, or if:

- They are between the ages of 18 and 19 and are still in high school.
- They have a disability that began before the age of 22.

As the custodial parent, you must file for benefits on your child's behalf and show proof that you have the right to do so, such as the child's birth certificate or adoption paperwork. You will also need to provide both your child's and your own Social Security number, and if you're applying for death benefits, you must provide a copy of the deceased parent's death certificate.

UNIQUE CIRCUMSTANCES FOR DISABLED WORKERS

It's difficult to increase SSDI benefits, but there are a few ways to do so. The SSA will automatically recalculate your benefits every year to account for cost-of-living increases. In addition, if you or your caseworker finds a clerical error or that you had additional earnings that were overlooked in your original application, the SSA will automatically increase or decrease your benefits.

You can't take disability and retirement benefits at the same time, but you can get retirement benefits if you are disabled, either by applying early or waiting until your full retirement age. If you don't claim benefits early, your disability benefits will automatically be converted to retirement benefits when you reach your full retirement age.

There are a few things you can do to increase either your retirement or your disability benefit:

Work for 35 years: Your retirement benefits are based on a 35-year work history, but if you don't work for that long, they will be calculated based on the years you did work. If you can, work for 35 years or more to increase the amount of your retirement benefit—however, if you are on SSDI or SSI, keep in mind that you cannot earn more than a certain amount without losing part or all of your disability benefits.

- **Don't apply for disability benefits until you reach the full retirement age:** At this point, your disability benefit will be equal to your full retirement benefit. The advantage of waiting this long is that you can work full-time without penalty, so you may have a higher benefit amount than you would if you'd been on disability for most of your adult life.
- **Apply for spousal retirement benefits:** have a disability. You will receive a lower benefit amount if you apply before reaching the full retirement age.
- **If you are widowed, apply for survivor benefits:** You can receive survivor and disability benefits at the same time. For that, you must have worked and paid into the system at some point to qualify for survivor benefits.
- **Hire a disability attorney:** An attorney experienced in this area of law can go over your documentation and find ways to maximize your benefits that you may not have been aware of.

If you are disabled, there are several options to maximize your benefits, but what if your income is extremely low or high?

Low-paid workers may find it challenging to delay their benefits until they reach or pass their full retirement age. If you're having trouble making ends meet, consider these options:

- **Monitor earnings carefully:** You might want to cut back on your hours so that you don't earn more than what you're allowed to while taking early retirement benefits.
- **Check for mistakes:** Read over your Social Security statements carefully. If you find mistakes in how much you earned or how much you are owed, contact the SSA immediately and report the error. You might get a recalculation in your favor!
- **Suspend your payments:** If you have been receiving benefits for less than a year, you have the right to change your mind and ask the SSA to cancel your claim. If your income increases or you decide you want to delay benefits after all, this is a viable option for you.

High-income earners have a cap on their payments. In 2023, no one can receive more than $4,555 per month even if they delay claiming retirement benefits until after age 70; those who retire when they reach the age of 67 cannot receive more than $3,627/month; and early claimants cannot receive more than $2,572/month. Keep this in mind if you have an unusually high income—it may be to your advantage to work fewer years if your early or full retirement benefits will be sufficient.

Both low and high-paid workers should speak to a tax attorney as part of their decision-making process, as adding benefits to wages can push you into a higher tax bracket, and if you bring in more than $25,000/year, your Social Security benefits become taxable.

HOW DISABILITY BENEFITS ARE CALCULATED

Both retirement and disability benefits are calculated based on how much money you earn while you are working. The SSA takes an average of your annual salaries. For retirement benefits, this is based on your top-earning salaries received over 35 years; for disability benefits, a slightly different formula is used that calculates your benefits based on your top-earning salaries in the years up to when you became disabled. This means that even if you don't claim disability until 10 years after you became disabled, the SSA will still calculate salaries up to the year you first became unable to work. It also drops, or declines to count, one to five years of your history, based on how long you worked before you became disabled.

The precise formula is complex, but the point is that your earnings, prior to your disability, and your age will determine your monthly benefit amount. In addition, for disability benefits, a portion of any income you still earn each month will be subtracted from your benefit amount. This is not the case with retirement benefits unless you retire early. If you take retirement benefits between the ages of 62 and 67, a portion of any income you earn will be counted against them.

If you receive survivor benefits, they are usually calculated based on your late partner's earnings. However, if your partner had already claimed early retirement benefits at the time of their death, you will receive only a partial benefit.

ADDITIONAL SPECIAL CIRCUMSTANCES TO CONSIDER

One of the top issues that retirees face is figuring out their finances, especially given the complexity of tax laws and requirements to make mandatory withdrawals from IRAs after they reach a certain age (for 2023, that age is six months past their 70th birthday).

We will discuss financial planning in Chapter 8; you may want to jump ahead to that information so that you have the best chance of getting a handle on your finances. It also helps to hire a financial planner with expertise in tax laws, retirement accounts, and related issues.

Another issue you may face is the amount of time it takes to process a disability claim. The system is set up so that only people who meet strict guidelines receive the disability income; a side effect of this type of vetting is that the process is extremely slow, and some people who do qualify are initially turned away.

If you are homeless, at risk of homelessness, or suffer from serious illness, the SSA will expedite your claim. Those with serious diseases will be processed under the "Compassionate Allowance (CAL) program." You do not need to do anything special to apply for this program; your caseworker will automatically refer your application for expedition if you mention your illness on the forms.

As mentioned above, some types of disability qualify for a "presumptive disability (PD) determination." This means that you will get payments immediately while your claim is still being processed, and you can keep that money even if the SSA later declines your claim. Similarly, if you are facing a financial emergency, you may be able to get an advanced payment while waiting for your claim to be processed. This is a one-time payment based on federal rates and may not exceed $999. This payment will be deducted from any regular SSI payment you become entitled to in the future.

If you have a terminal illness, such as metastasized cancer with no hope of remission, your caseworker will refer it to the Terminal Illness program and expedite your claim.

Military veterans are also eligible for expedited claims:

- Those who have been rated as 100% permanently disabled by the Veterans Administration (VA).
- Those who are "wounded warriors," meaning they were seriously injured in the line of duty, but are not 100% permanently disabled.

If the VA has made this determination, you should put it on your disability application so that it may be expedited. You may also need to provide documentation from your VA doctor.

If you are in "dire need," meaning you are extremely low-income and are homeless, or about to become homeless, you can apply for an expedited hearing. You will need a letter of dire need, explaining the circumstances, and as much evidence of need as possible. For example, eviction notices from your landlord or a letter from the director of a homeless shelter where you are staying can demonstrate your lack of stable housing. If you have high medical bills because of an illness or injury, attach copies of those bills to your application as well.

Finally, if the SSA is notified that an applicant is a threat to themselves or to other people, they will notify the appropriate authorities as well as expedite the claim. The SSA is committed to the safety of applicants and people the applicant may come in contact with.

QUIZ YOURSELF

Answer the following questions to test your knowledge of special circumstances:

- Which benefit is designed for disabled adults who have had that disability since childhood?

  a) SSDI
  b) Child's Disability Benefits
  c) Survivor Benefits
  d) Compassionate Allowance Program

- Children must have developed their disability before the age of __ to qualify for Child Disability Benefits.

  a) 12
  b) 5
  c) 22
  d) 18

- After you submit your application, how long will you have to wait to begin receiving disability benefits?

  a) Not at all—it's immediate
  b) Three to six months, but if you have special circumstances, you may receive an expedited application
  c) Three to six months, unless you are in dire need or have a

serious disability that allows you to get provisional payments

d) Both B and C

- What is the time you may have to wait before you receive disability benefits called?

a) Time-wasting period

b) Evaluation period

c) Delayed start of benefits

d) Waiting period

- What type of work must an individual NOT be able to do to qualify for disability?

a) No kind of work at all is allowed

b) Working on a computer

c) Standing on their feet

d) Substantial gainful work

Answers:

1) B

2) C

3) D

4) D

5) D

SUMMARY

In this chapter, we looked at special circumstances where you may be eligible for assistance from the SSA.

Disability is a big one. The SSA offers two disability programs, depending on the extent of the disability and whether the person has ever been able to work. Severely disabled children, meaning people under the age of 18 whose abilities are limited by their condition, may qualify for the Child Disability Program, which pays a monthly stipend. Adults over the age of 18 who have had a disability since childhood may also qualify for this program. Adults may also qualify for SSDI, which pays a monthly stipend to adults who may be able to work on a limited basis.

The process for applying for disability benefits involves filling out an application, attaching supporting documentation, and waiting. If you have a medical condition, it is important to attach a doctor's note; you might also need to attach proof of dire circumstances, such as an eviction notice, and if you are applying on behalf of a child, you must also provide their birth certificate or adoption paperwork. Finally, if you are applying for survivor benefits, you must attach the appropriate death certificate. Children may be entitled to survivor benefits until they turn 18. If they are still in high school upon their 18th birthday, they can extend the benefits until they graduate.

It normally takes three to six months for a disability application to be processed, but there are special circumstances in which your application might be expedited or you may receive advance payments before your application is approved. If you have a severe disability or illness, are homeless or about to become homeless, or have sustained disabling injuries in the line of duty, your application may be expedited. You will need to note these circumstances when you apply.

We have learned a lot together about Social Security! In the next and final chapter, we will discuss how to put it all together to create a comprehensive plan for your retirement.

Turn the page when you are ready.

The Missing Guidebook

"He who wishes to secure the good of others,
has already secured his own." – Confucius

Social security (and every other government program for that matter) should come with a guidebook. There are so many people who don't get the support they're entitled to simply because the system is too complicated to navigate and they aren't sure what their rights are or how to access the help they need.

RetireWise aims to be the guidebook they forgot to write – so people like you can get what they deserve and step into retirement without the stress, safe in the knowledge that their families will be provided for and they'll have the funds to pursue their goals long after they receive their last paycheck.

The problem now is, since this guidance isn't built into the system, how can we make sure that the people who need it find the help they're looking for?

The answer is as simple as word of mouth – and you can help hundreds more people like you access what they're entitled to simply by leaving a short review.

By leaving a review of this book on Amazon, you'll show everyone who's searching for help with navigating the system exactly where they can find all the guidance they need.

Reviews make it easy for readers to find the resources they're looking for... and in this case, that's going to help them access the retirement they've been dreaming of.

Thank you for your support. Social security may not come with a guidebook, but together, we can fill that gap.

5

THE ABCDS OF MEDICARE - NAVIGATING YOUR WAY TO BETTER HEALTH

Medicare is known as the health care program for seniors, but did you know it's not a "one-size-fits-all" offer? Understanding the various moving parts of this program could be your key to a healthy and happy retirement. Medicare's complexity can be confusing; it's easy to overlook something extremely crucial and subsequently fail to claim all the benefits you're entitled to.

Let's simplify the program together.

MEDICARE BASICS

As you may know, Lyndon Johnson signed Medicare into law for the first time in 1965 so that retirees could have access to appropriate health care, regardless of their medical needs. However, the seeds of this program were planted 20 years earlier by Harry Truman. Truman wanted to create a federally-funded program that would guarantee every citizen's ability to access appropriate health care, no matter their income level. And Truman wasn't the first to think of the idea either—Teddy Roosevelt envisioned a national healthcare system when he ran for President as a third-party candidate in 1912.

Truman and Roosevelt envisioned a system that paid for ALL Americans' healthcare needs, something that progressive politicians such as Bernie Sanders and Elizabeth Warren still want to enact today. While no such program exists as of 2023, Medicare does offer government-sponsored health insurance to those over the age of 65, and Truman and his wife were the first Medicare recipients.

Enacting this program was one of John F. Kennedy's priorities. He learned that 56% of people over the age of 65 did not have adequate healthcare coverage, and therefore strongly pushed for legislation to change that (Medicare, 2022). After Kennedy's death, Johnson continued the push and managed to get Medicare signed into law. It ultimately went into effect in 1966.

As of 2022, nearly 65 million people are enrolled in Medicare Part A, and Medicare accounts for 20% of the federal budget. Politicians worry that the trust fund for Medicare will be depleted by 2028. If this happens, payroll taxes may be levied to pay for Medicare, just as these taxes are used to fund Social Security.

TODAY'S MEDICARE HAS FOUR PARTS

Medicare has four parts that cover different aspects of health care:

- **Part A** covers in-patient care. This is care that you receive in a hospital, such as surgery and recovery from surgery, emergency care, or severe illnesses requiring hospitalization.

- **Part B** covers all other medical treatments. It has been expanded over the years to cover things such as end-stage renal disease for people younger than 65.
- **Part C** is what's known as Medicare Advantage. This is a program that participants buy into. Like private insurance, Medicare Advantage requires premium payments as well as co-pays and deductibles.
- **Part D** is prescription drug coverage. Participants are subject to restrictions on what drugs are covered.

Medicare Part A is paid for through employment taxes; usually, enrollees do not have to pay monthly premiums. However, those who have never worked, or are otherwise ineligible, may have to pay monthly premiums of up to $506 as of 2023. If you fall into this category and do not buy in when you turn 65, you may have to pay a penalty.

As with private insurance, Medicare Part A offers coverage only for services the insurer deems medically necessary. As of 2023, these services include some home health aide services and hospice services. However, these services are only available to those who meet certain criteria, such as being homebound or being diagnosed with a terminal illness that reduces life expectancy to six months or less. Some types of care, such as in-patient hospital stays, may require deductibles to be met before any coverage kicks in.

You are eligible for Medicare Part A if you

- are over the age of 65 and receive Social Security or Railroad Board Benefits.
- are younger than 65 but receiving Railroad Board or Social Security disability benefits.

- are younger than 65 and have a diagnosis of amyotrophic lateral sclerosis.

If you are over 65 and not claiming retirement benefits, or you are under the age of 65 and have a diagnosis of ESRD (ESRD patients can get Medicare at any age), you must sign up for Medicare Part A, instead of being enrolled automatically.

If you do not qualify for premium-free Medicare, you may enroll when you turn 65 or during any enrollment periods. If you do not enroll when you first qualify, you may be subject to a 10% increase in premiums when you do enroll.

All other programs are optional and thus require premium payments. Part B is a lower-cost program than private insurance programs and works quite similarly, covering needed health care outside of hospitalization such as doctors' visits, diagnostic tests, and medications. Chemotherapy and similar treatments are covered under this plan. You only pay co-pays until you meet your deductible. As of 2023, the deductible is $226.

We will discuss Medicare Part C more thoroughly in the next section. Medicare Part C is an alternative coverage program; and Medicare enrollees choose between this and Medicare Parts A and B rather than signing up for both.

Medicare Part D offers prescription benefits. If you have Medicare Parts A and B, you will pay an additional premium for this coverage. If you have Medicare Part C, it typically covers the premium on Part D. There are limits to how much drug coverage you get through Part D; you will pay out-of-pocket once you reach this limit. However, there is a cap on the amount you will be responsible for.

Let's look at an example to make this clearer. Suppose your Part D coverage has a limit of $5,000 and a cap of $1,500—these numbers are made up; real coverage is likely much different. If you are prescribed drugs that cost more than $5,000 within a calendar year, you will have to pay out-of-pocket for any other drugs that are prescribed. However, if you spend more than $1,500 out-of-pocket, you will no longer be required to pay out-of-pocket for additional drugs. Instead, you will pay a co-pay on all additional medicines for the year.

If your Medicare plans don't cover all your medical needs, you can purchase Medigap insurance. This is a private insurance that covers services that Medicare does not.

MEDICARE VS. MEDICARE ADVANTAGE

Medicare Part C is known as Medicare Advantage. This is a program that you buy into, but how else does it differ from basic Medicare?

Medicare and Medicare Advantage cover different things. Original Medicare requires you to get three different types of coverage. Part A covers hospital stays, Part B covers other medical care, and Part D covers prescriptions. Conversely, Medicare Advantage offers coverage of all three aspects of health care. This means you only have to buy into one program. However, it's important to bear in mind that Medicare Advantage is not provided by the federal government. Instead, it is provided by private health insurance companies that have partnered with the government. Thus, the costs may be higher and you may be subject to more limits as to which doctors and services are covered.

That said, Medicare Advantage may offer coverage that basic Medicare does not, including:

- dental coverage
- vision coverage
- hearing aids and other hearing coverage
- transportation to and from the doctor's office (often through a door-to-door car or van service)

Considering whether you want or need these additional services can help make it clearer to you which plan is best for you. It's also important to consider your total costs when making this decision. When comparing costs, it's important to keep a few things in mind.

First, Original Medicare requires you to sign up for three different programs, only one of which may be premium-free. Even if your Part A coverage doesn't require premiums, you will still be required to pay premium costs for Parts B and D. You will also need to consider the deductibles for each of these programs and the co-pays and coverage limits. All of these costs can easily add up.

Conversely, Medicare Advantage requires you to pay one premium rather than two or three. You will also have to meet only one deductible before coverage kicks in, though you still may need to pay a co-pay at many doctors' offices you might visit.

The biggest difference involves coverage. Original Medicare covers all US hospitals and doctor's offices, but does not offer any coverage in foreign countries. Medicare Advantage covers only in-network providers in the United States, but may offer limited coverage in some foreign countries.

If you are somebody who does not plan to travel much or who doesn't want to go outside of the United States, it may make more sense to opt for Original Medicare. However, if your retirement plans involve a lot of travel, especially to foreign countries, opting for Medicare Advantage may make more sense.

HOW MEDICARE WORKS WITH OTHER INSURANCE

Although Medicare is designed to make health care more affordable for seniors, it may not cover all costs. Some people may have secondary insurance to cover things that Medicare doesn't, while others might be reluctant to let go of their private health insurance.

If you have both Medicare and private health insurance, various rules govern how your health care is paid for.

When you have two types of insurance, one is considered primary, and the other is considered secondary. Whichever insurance is primary kicks in first. If you've exceeded coverage limits or your primary insurance doesn't cover services for some reason, your secondary insurance will be used to cover those costs.

Whether Medicare is your primary or secondary insurance depends on your situation:

- If you have insurance through your job, in most cases, that insurance will be primary, and Medicare will be secondary. However, if you work for a very small company (fewer than 20 employees), Medicare will be your primary insurance.

- Similarly, if you are on a job-based disability insurance, that insurance is primary unless your company has less than 100 employees.
- If you are using liability coverage, Medicare is secondary for all relevant claims, though Medicare will be your primary coverage for non-related claims. For example, if you fall at work, your liability insurance will take care of injury-related care, but Medicare will be primary for your routine health care.

Some insurance programs don't work with Medicare. In this case, you have to choose between them:

- You can either use VA benefits or Medicare, not both at the same visit.
- If you are not eligible for Medicare, you must use other retiree insurance.
- If you had Consolidated Omnibus Reconciliation Act insurance (COBRA) before becoming eligible for Medicare, you must use Medicare and cannot use COBRA.

If you are on a low income and have both Medicaid and Medicare, you may only use Medicaid for services that are not covered by Medicare.

YOUR MEDICARE CHECKLIST

Check off the following items to ensure that you understand each concept and how to maximize your Medicare benefits:

- Review the costs of Medicare vs. Medicare Advantage and decide which one to participate in.

- Enroll in Medicare Part A, B, and D or exclusively in Medicare Part C (Medicare Advantage).
- Receive your health insurance card and welcome packet. Read over all information carefully.
- Learn what your total premiums, deductibles, and co-pays are. Budget for these.

SUMMARY

Medicare is a government-paid healthcare program that is meant to help ensure that healthcare is affordable for retirees. This is important because as you get older, you may need more doctors' visits or treatments to deal with serious health issues.

The program was created in 1965, but progressive politicians have envisioned a health care program that covered all Americans' needs since Teddy Roosevelt ran for President as a third party in 1912. Medicare falls far short of this lofty goal, instead insuring most people over the age of 65. It is important to note that this program is not free to consumers, though premiums, co-pays, and deductibles are usually more affordable than private insurance.

There are two options when it comes to Medicare. You can enroll separately in Part A, B, and D, which cover your hospital stays, outpatient treatment, and prescription costs; conversely, you may elect Medicare Part C, also called Medicare Advantage, which covers all three. Except for Medicare Part A, all Medicare programs require you to pay monthly premiums, you will also have to pay deductibles and co-pays. Medicare Advantage requires you to see only in-network doctors, while you can see any doctor you want with Original Medicare.

When evaluating these programs, it's important to consider total costs and what services you need coverage for. In addition, if you want to travel, you should be aware that Medicare Advantage offers some coverage in foreign countries, while basic Medicare does not. Additionally, Medicare can be coordinated with most private insurance companies. In some cases, Medicare will be considered your primary insurance, meaning it'll be used first, while in other cases, it will not. You cannot use Medicare at the same time as VA Benefits, and if you have both Medicare and Medicaid, you cannot use Medicaid unless Medicare does not cover your service.

It's important to grasp these fundamentals, but equally important to ensure that you choose the optimal healthcare plan for yourself. We'll do a deep dive into different Medicare plans in the next chapter.

Turn the page to get started!

6

CHOOSE WISELY - YOUR GUIDE TO THE RIGHT MEDICARE PLAN

S electing the right Medicare plan is one of the most consequential choices you'll make. If you want to live the retirement of your dreams, you'll need the right coverage. Someone who wants to travel has different health care needs than a "homebody" who wants to make sure that medical expenses don't eat up all of their hard-earned retirement savings, and a person with any chronic health conditions needs different coverage than someone who only needs preventative health care.

Whatever your situation is, you deserve a retirement that is as peaceful, stress-free, and joyful as possible. Choosing the right Medicare plan can help you achieve that. This chapter will explore all the ins and outs of various Medicare plans so that you can make the best choice for yourself and your family.

REVIEWING THE DIFFERENT OPTIONS

As we discussed in the previous chapter, there are four parts to Medicare. Parts A, B, and D work together to provide you with different types of health care coverage; conversely, Part C, or Medicare Advantage, provides comprehensive coverage.

Here's a breakdown of the various programs again:

- **Part A** covers hospital stays.
- **Part B** covers outpatient treatment, such as doctor's visits.
- **Part C** is comprehensive coverage that includes hospital visits, outpatient treatment, and prescription drug coverage.
- **Part D** covers most prescriptions.

Now let's look at each program in more depth.

PART A: WHAT EXACTLY IS COVERED IF I HAVE TO BE HOSPITALIZED?

First and foremost, Part A covers hospital stays. If your doctor says you need to be hospitalized, in most cases, your hospitalization will be covered. That means that hospitalizations for severe illness, planned or unplanned surgeries and recovery, and emergency room visits are all covered.

There are also a few ancillary services that are covered by Part A:

- Temporary stays in nursing facilities or nursing homes following hospitalization, if ordered by a doctor.
- Home health care services prescribed by your doctor, such as physical or occupational therapy.

- Hospice care for those with a terminal illness who are not expected to survive for more than six months.

However, this doesn't mean that all services are free; you may have to pay out-of-pocket until you hit your deductible or pay co-pays for some services. However, these costs are usually cheaper than what private insurance requires. Your co-pays are usually about 20% of the cost of service., and if you do have to pay a premium, it will vary based on your income level.

PART B: OUTPATIENT TREATMENT COVERAGE

Part B covers all other medical services. This includes all of your doctor's visits; whether you are having a preventative check-up with your general practitioner or seeing a specialist to help you manage a specific health condition, Medicare Part B will cover it. However, as of 2023, Medicare Part B does not cover most dental, vision, or hearing services, though it may cover some diagnostic exams, and some eye surgeries such as cataract removal procedures.

In addition to doctor's visits, Part B covers some services you might not expect:

- participation in clinical research studies (some costs related to the study may be covered)
- durable medical equipment such as walkers, canes, wheelchairs, and oxygen tanks
- mental health services
- certain prescription drugs that must be administered by a healthcare provider
- some ambulance rides

Part B coverage is optional, which means you won't be penalized if you elect not to take it when you turn 65. You will have to pay a small premium each month for this coverage.

WHAT DOES MEDICARE ADVANTAGE COVER?

Medicare Advantage offers comprehensive coverage, which means that hospital stays, outpatient treatment, and most prescription drugs are covered by one plan. You have to pay for the plan, and you can only see doctors that are in your network. As with private insurance, you may need referrals to see specialists or pre-authorizations for certain treatments or tests. You also have a choice of plans: Medicare Advantage consists of private insurance companies that have contracted with Medicare to provide services at reduced rates.

Unlike Original Medicare, Medicare Advantage covers vision, dental, and hearing services.

In addition, there are a few other benefits to Medicare Advantage:

- wellness services
- adult daycare services
- transportation to doctors' visits (usually a car or van service that picks you up at your door and drops you off at home after your appointment)

Medicare Advantage also offers limited coverage in foreign countries, making it a better option for you if you plan to do a lot of traveling.

ARE ALL PRESCRIPTIONS COVERED?

Although Part B is optional, you can't get Part D coverage unless you are first enrolled in both Parts A and B.

Part D covers prescription drugs. Most drugs are covered, but the exact list differs depending on which Part D plan you choose. You can get a list of approved drugs from your Part D provider.

If you have diabetes, Part D will usually cover your medication and testing supplies. In 2023, a new $35 cap on insulin went into effect, meaning that Medicare recipients will not pay more than this amount for insulin under any Part D plan.

Technically, you can enroll in Part D anytime, as the coverage is optional. However, if you choose not to enroll when you turn 65, you may incur penalties for late enrollment if you sign up later. Bear in mind that you do not need Part D if you have Medicare Advantage, as prescriptions are covered under that plan.

MEDIGAP COVERAGE

If you've ever seen Medicare plans with other letters of the alphabet besides A through D, those are Medigap plans. Medigap is a type of supplemental insurance you can buy to cover services that Medicare doesn't, such as hearing, vision, or dental services.

You pay monthly premiums for Medigap services, and you can choose from several providers who offer them. Each plan is slightly different than the others and covers different services, but the plan type you purchase will be the same no matter who the provider is. For example, if you purchase Medigap Plan M, it will cover the same services no matter who you buy it from, but Plan N will cover different services than Plan M.

You cannot use Medigap insurance with Medicare Advantage, which is also a private insurance program meant to cover various services.

SHOULD I ENROLL IN MEDICARE ADVANTAGE?

There are pros and cons to Medicare Advantage; you should consider these carefully before making a final decision.

+ *Pros:*

- **Everything is covered through the same plan:** You won't have to keep track of deductibles and premiums for two or three separate plans, as you would if you signed up for Original Medicare Parts A, B, and D along with any supplemental Medigap insurance you need.
- **It may be cheaper:** Your premiums for Original Medicare Parts B and D usually take a bigger bite out of your monthly budget than Medicare Advantage.
- **There are caps on out-of-pocket costs:** You won't pay more than $8,300/year in out-of-pocket costs if you use in-network doctors.
- **More plan options that may fit your individual needs better:** Medicare Advantage has various types of plan structures. For example, you can choose a PPO if you want more options for seeing out-of-network doctors or an SNP if you need coverage for chronic health conditions
- **Vision, dental, and hearing may be covered, depending on your plan:** Original Medicare does not cover these supplementary services, which many older Americans might need help with.

- **There is coordination between different healthcare providers:** Medicare Advantage may facilitate coordination between your general practitioner and any specialists that you see, which can make it easier for you to get the comprehensive health care you need.
- **There is some coverage in foreign countries:** If you plan to travel outside of the United States, you'll need coverage in case of a medical emergency; Medicare Advantage provides this, while Original Medicare does not.

— *Cons:*

- **Restrictions on which doctors you can see:** While Original Medicare covers most doctors throughout the country, Medicare Advantage requires you to see doctors within a particular network. If you see an out-of-network doctor, you will pay more out-of-pocket and may not have any part of your service covered, depending on your plan type.
- **More red tape:** As with private insurance, you may need to get referrals or pre-authorizations before some services are covered. This can make it harder to get appropriate care, and if you have a condition in which time is precious, this could be a problem.
- **Your network may not remain stable:** Your network can change at any time. Providers can leave a practice or a practice can leave the network, which can leave you scrambling to find new providers to meet your needs.
- **Some services may not be available where you live:** If you need a highly specialized service, there may not be any in-network providers where you live and you may have to go out of state to get the care you need.

- **The choices can be overwhelming:** While having a lot of plan types leads to greater flexibility, you also may become overwhelmed and have a hard time deciding which coverage you need.

HOW TO CHOOSE THE PLAN THAT IS RIGHT FOR YOU

The first decision that you must make is whether you will choose Original Medicare or Medicare Advantage. To make this decision, you should consider several factors.

First, compare the total costs for each program. Remember to factor in your estimated premiums, co-pay amounts, and deductible amounts to determine how much each plan will cost you. You also want to consider your healthcare needs and what you anticipate needing in the future. If you are in good health and not on any medications, you may be tempted to skip Medicare Part D. But enrolling later could be more expensive; does your family or personal medical history suggest you'll need extensive medications later? Or does it make more sense to get Medicare Advantage now so that your prescriptions will be covered in the future without having to purchase additional insurance?

If you currently wear glasses or hearing aids, or you have gum disease or other serious dental issues, Medicare Advantage may be a better option for you, as this plan covers all dental, vision, and hearing-related services. Original Medicare does cover some related services, such as eye exams, but does not cover materials such as glasses or contacts. However, another option may be to get Original Medicare and purchase an appropriate Medigap supplement to cover these services. In addition, you may want to talk to your dentist, eye doctor, or hearing specialist; some offices have payment plans or in-office insurance plans that may save you money. If this is the case, you could use the in-office insurance to pay for these services and Original Medicare for your medical care. Chronic health conditions are also a genuine concern. If you have prediabetes or diabetes, you'll need to be able to get specialized care to help you manage your condition.

If there's any reason that you are concerned about finding a doctor that meets your needs, you may find the in-network requirements of Medicare Advantage to be too limiting. In this case, Original Medicare may give you more options, although you should consider whether a PPO—which allows you to go out of network to an extent—might be a feasible option for you. You should also consider your lifestyle. If you plan on doing a lot of traveling, you'll want to go with Medicare Advantage, as it offers limited coverage in foreign countries. Alternatively, you may find it cheaper to purchase supplemental private insurance for your travels to use in coordination with Original Medicare.

Finally, you'll want to consider customer service. If a particular Medicare provider's office is hard to reach by telephone or email, the people staffing the phone lines are rude, or you don't think they do a good job of explaining policy decisions, these factors will cause unnecessary stress for you. If this is the first time you've used Medicare, you won't know what the customer service is like; however, you can read reviews of different providers or plan managers before you decide who to sign up with.

You may have to wait for an open enrollment period to enroll in certain parts of the program, so keep that in mind when making decisions.

SUMMARY

Medicare is complicated, partially because there are so many plans and options to choose from. But once you understand all the options, you'll find it a lot easier to make a decision.

There are two types of Medicare most people consider: Original Medicare or Medicare Advantage. The only part of Original Medicare that is mandatory is Part A, which covers hospitalization, temporary stays in nursing or rehabilitation facilities, and hospice care for those with short life expectancies. Part A is premium-free for most retirees, but you will still have to pay co-pays and deductibles. Optionally, you can also sign up for Part B coverage, which pays for adult daycare programs and wellness programs as well as most doctor's visits; or/and Part D, which covers most drug prescriptions. Both Part B and Part D require monthly premium payments, which vary based on your income level, as well as requiring you to meet a deductible before your coverage kicks in.

Alternatively, you can sign up for Part C, or Medicare Advantage. Medicare Advantage allows you to choose an insurance plan among those offered by private companies that have partnered with Medicare. These plans work like traditional insurance; you have to get referrals from your general practitioner to see a specialist and must see an in-network doctor on most plans. This is more limiting than Original Medicare, which allows you to see almost any doctor in the United States. However, Medicare Advantage offers limited coverage in foreign countries, while Original Medicare offers none. In addition, some people prefer the convenience of having one type of insurance to cover all their needs rather than purchasing several different policies, as happens with Original Medicare. Finally, Medicare Advantage may offer dental, vision, and hearing coverage, which Original Medicare does not, and also offers additional benefits such as door-to-door transportation to medical facilities. If you have Original Medicare, you may need to purchase Medigap insurance to cover services that your Medicare does not. Medigap offers several different programs, so you must pay careful attention to ensure you're purchasing the one that most meets your needs.

In order to determine which program is right for you, compare the total costs, including premiums, co-pays, and deductibles. You'll also want to consider your current healthcare needs as well as what you anticipate you may need in the future. Finally, you'll need to consider your lifestyle. For example, coverage in foreign countries will be more important to a frequent traveler than to someone who plans to spend their retirement at home with their grandchildren. You'll also want to consider what services are available in your area, as there may be few in-network doctors in your town or city. It can be helpful to start a reflective journal while researching and enrolling in Medicare. Journaling regularly can help you organize and clarify your thoughts and make the best decision for yourself.

Healthcare can be one of the more expensive aspects of retirement. Although Medicare can help defray costs, in most cases, you'll still have to pay something toward doctor's visits, prescriptions, and hospital stays. That's why it's so important to learn how to manage your healthcare costs when you are planning your retirement.

The next chapter will help you do that.

7

SECURING YOUR HEALTH - CONTROLLING COSTS IN RETIREMENT

Healthcare is expensive, especially for retirees. According to the Fidelity Retiree Health Care Cost Estimate (2023), the average 65-year-old American will require almost $157,500 saved to cover their health care expenses after their retirement. The average married couple in this age bracket needs over $300,000.

Retirees often have higher healthcare costs because of chronic conditions, such as diabetes, that may begin in older adulthood. But even if you are in perfect health, preventative costs such as tests and check-ups add up, and you may also have a lot of medications that you need to purchase every month.

While some healthcare costs are unavoidable—going to the doctor is not optional if you want to maximize your health and longevity—there are some ways to save. Throughout this chapter, we will discuss how to plan and minimize healthcare costs during your retirement.

RISING HEALTHCARE COSTS AMONG SENIORS

Healthcare costs are rising exponentially, and a big part of that burden tends to fall on older people. Between 1970 and 2009, healthcare costs rose from five to ten percent of most Western countries' GDP (Meijer et al, 2013).

Social scientists differ on why this is happening, but one thing is clear: people are living longer than ever before. That means there are more people using healthcare services than in the past, which leads to an increased need for both Medicare and private health insurance. Older people may have more health problems; in addition, they may utilize more preventative services to protect their health.

There are also several other factors that influence healthcare spending:

- New medical technology can enable people to live longer, happier lives and cure or treat diseases that were previously deemed fatal. However, this technology is often expensive, and healthcare providers must pay for it somehow.
- The way the healthcare system is organized makes a difference. In the United States, where there is no national health insurance plan (except for Medicare for people over the age of 65), healthcare costs have skyrocketed. Conversely, other Western countries must find a way to pay for their national health insurance programs and may need to raise taxes to accommodate the greater number of people using them.

- The general state of the economy will influence prices for everything, including healthcare. If wages or prices go up, healthcare costs will, too.

What does this mean for you? Basically, you are part of an aging population that is facing higher healthcare costs than previous generations did. Healthcare is a necessity, so you can't cut back on it, but you do need to ensure that costs stay under control as much as possible.

One of the biggest challenges involves managing chronic conditions. The National Council of Aging has found that 95% of people over the age of 55 have, at least, one chronic condition (NCOA, 2023). Chronic conditions are more costly to treat because they require ongoing monitoring and treatment. For example, diabetes costs an average of $20,000/year per patient, while Alzheimer's and dementia cost about $49,000.

However, there are some solutions:

- **Online monitoring of some conditions:** It may be cheaper for people to track conditions like diabetes from the comfort of their homes and upload information to their patient portal for their doctors to see. Similarly, some conditions require only virtual visits rather than seeing the doctor in person.
- **Community-based care services:** They can reduce the need for long-term care, which will save money. Long-term care is costly, so anything that can reduce people's dependence on it can help cut costs.
- **Focus on preventative services:** The more people can take action to stay healthy, the lower the costs will be.

Treatment of serious conditions is far more costly than wellness visits, after all.

The best way to reduce healthcare costs in the future involves using digital technology, but paradoxically, many older people find it difficult to use these innovative options. Thus, it is incumbent upon leaders in the healthcare industry to ensure that all tech is user-friendly, and that there are services available to help older people learn how to use these new technologies.

VARIABLES INFLUENCING HEALTHCARE SPENDING

Healthcare costs are rising in the United States and have been for decades. Probasco (2023) theorizes that one reason for the rising costs is the existence of services like Medicare, as providers are aware that government-paid insurance will pay any amount. However, this theory does not explain why the United States has higher healthcare costs than other Western nations, when it's the only one without a national health insurance plan for all citizens.

The state of the American healthcare system is grim. In 2020, Americans spent more than their peers on healthcare, yet had the highest COVID mortality rate, the highest rates of infant and maternal mortality, and lower life expectancies (Probasco, 2023). Thirty one percent of those increased costs came from hospitalizations, suggesting that preventative care can help cut costs. Some of the factors influencing healthcare costs therefore include:

- a rising population
- a larger number of aging seniors, including those with greater longevity than earlier generations
- an increase in chronic conditions

- an increase in how many people are using medical services

COVID-19 contributed initially to many of these costs; however, long term, the disease's presence isn't expected to dramatically increase healthcare costs.

The No Surprise Act of 2021 may help lower costs, as it outlaws surprise medical bills and requires transparency on the part of insurance companies about how costs are calculated.

STRATEGIES TO COPE WITH UNEXPECTED MEDICAL EXPENSES

No matter how healthy you are, you may face a medical emergency or other unexpected healthcare expenses. While you can't control the costs of healthcare, there are things you can do to minimize the financial impact of unplanned medical treatment. One of the most powerful tools in your financial arsenal is your "emergency fund." This is a savings account specifically for emergencies—once you put money into it, you should not take it out unless you are in dire need.

If you're going to use an emergency fund, it's important for you to have clear definitions of what constitutes an emergency. It can be tempting to remove money from the account for "emergency" needs that are really just wants, such as not being able to afford tickets to a once-in-a-lifetime experience, but if you do this, you won't be covered during a bona fide emergency.

Here are some typical examples of emergencies:

- You or your partner unexpectedly lose a job and need to pay bills.

- You lose wages because you have a serious illness and are out of work for a month.
- Your car breaks down, and you have no other way to pay for repairs.
- A global event disrupts your livelihood for an indefinite period of time, such as the COVID-19 lockdowns in early 2020.

These types of unforeseen circumstances require you to spend money you don't have on basic needs. Thus, without an emergency fund, you may be left with little recourse. It's best to save money regularly for emergencies. Many financial advisors suggest saving three to six months' worth of income. But how do you do it?

One way is to budget a certain percentage of every check you get for emergencies. For example, if you are receiving Social Security income, you could put 10% of each check into savings. If you use this method, make sure you still have enough money in your checking account to cover your expenses so that you won't have to take money out of your emergency fund any time soon. If your budget allows, you could set up an auto transfer on certain days of the month. That way, your bank automatically moves money into your savings. Just make sure you have the money in your account on the day of the transfer so that you don't incur overdraft fees.

If money is tight, look closely at your budget to see where you can cut back on your spending. You could also look for ways to increase your income, such as selling unneeded items or getting a second job, so that you can afford to put good money into emergency savings.

SHOULD YOU CONSIDER LONG-TERM CARE INSURANCE?

If you're concerned about paying for nursing homes or other long-term healthcare needs, you might want to consider purchasing insurance to cover it. Although many people think of nursing homes when considering long-term care, that's far from the only thing this type of insurance covers. Seventy three percent of people receive long-term care services at home (US Bank, 2022), and this type of insurance covers the cost of home health aides as well as assisted living facilities or nursing homes. If you should become ill or disabled enough to require this kind of care, having insurance can help defray costs so you don't need to use your retirement savings or depend on your family to take care of you.

While you may not want to pay for an additional insurance policy on top of your Medicare, the fact is that Medicare does not cover most long-term care. Medicare Part A will cover a short-term stay in a nursing facility, following treatment in a hospital, but if you need more than 100 days' worth of care, you or your family will have to pay out-of-pocket unless you have long-term care insurance.

Even if you are in perfect health, you may still want to consider long-term care. Sadly, the majority of people end up needing it as they approach the end of their lives, and if you don't have insurance, this type of care can eat into your savings, and if you run out of money, you won't be able to pay for your care.

Costs vary depending on your age and health, the policy, and what it covers. Many policies offer limited benefits; however, you can purchase policies that are more expansive. You might also consider a hybrid life/long-term care policy that allows you to make claims against the policy for long-term care and offers your beneficiaries a cash benefit from what's left after you pass away.

USING MEDIGAP OR MEDICARE ADVANTAGE TO LOWER HEALTHCARE COSTS

Depending on your Medicare plan, you might be able to use it to lower your healthcare costs. If you have Original Medicare, you may also want to purchase Medigap supplemental insurance. As we discussed in Chapter 5, there are various Medigap plans available to cover needs that Medicare does not. It's important to examine all available plans and choose the one that best meets your needs, as not all plans cover the same services.

You do not need Medigap insurance if you have Medicare Advantage—in fact, you cannot use both at once, and it is illegal for anyone to try to sell you Medigap if you are already enrolled in Medicare Advantage. Medicare Advantage is similar to private insurance and covers many services Original Medicare does not, so it would be redundant to also purchase a Medigap policy (even if you could do so).

If you already have Medigap insurance and switch to Medicare Advantage, you won't be able to use your Medigap plan anymore. You can cancel it even if you're unsure whether you will stay with Medicare Advantage. If, within the first 12 months, you decide not to stay with Medicare Advantage, you have the right to switch back and get the same Medigap plan you had before.

CREATE YOUR HEALTHCARE COST WORKSHEET

Now that you understand a bit more about the different factors contributing to rising healthcare costs and how to manage them, it's time to create your healthcare cost worksheet.

Fill in the following to figure out what your current and future healthcare costs may be:

CURRENT EXPENSES

Health Insurance

Primary Insurance Premium: _____

Secondary Insurance Premium: _____

Annual deductibles (medical): _____

Out-of-Pocket Expenses

Co-pays for routine visits: _____

Co-pays for prescription drugs: _____

Non-covered medicines: _____

Non-covered dental care: _____

Non-covered vision care: _____

Non-covered hearing care: _____

Other non-covered medical care (e.g., specialists, experimental treatments, etc.):

_____

Total current expenses:

PREDICTED FUTURE EXPENSES

Chronic-condition-related care:

Cost of long-term care (should I need it):

Total predicted future expenses:

SAVINGS OPTIONS

Amount of medical expenses 100% covered by Medicare or other insurance: _____

Amount currently saved in Emergency Fund:

Total Savings:

SUBTRACT Total Savings from (Current + Future Expenses). This is how much you must save to prepare for future healthcare costs.

Check savings from various insurance programs to see how this number changes.

SUMMARY

Healthcare is expensive, especially if you are a senior citizen living in the United States. Costs rise every year and will continue to rise, and it's hard to cut back spending on these types of expenses since you need health care for your survival.

There are many reasons for health care to be as expensive as it is today. One of the biggest reasons is that people are living longer. This means there are more people in need of services; in addition, older people may need more healthcare than younger people. Older people often need more medical treatment for various diseases, including chronic conditions such as diabetes. However, they may also take greater advantage of preventative services, adding to the cost of healthcare.

Another reason for rising healthcare costs may be that government programs give people greater access to healthcare, which puts a bigger burden on the system. However, Americans pay far more for healthcare than countries that have a national healthcare system, so government programs can't fully explain this phenomenon. Indeed, the United States has poorer healthcare outcomes than many other countries despite far higher costs for healthcare. Greater utilization of services is only one factor contributing to the cost of healthcare; the bigger reasons are linked to the fact that today's population is larger than it has ever been before.

If you want to lower your healthcare costs, the best thing you can do for yourself is start an emergency fund. You can start this fund anytime during your life, but the sooner you begin, the better. The key to successful emergency savings is understanding what you can and cannot use the money for. It's important to keep it in the fund unless you have a true emergency, such as losing a job or your wages being reduced due to an extended hospital stay.

In addition to having an emergency fund with three to six months' worth of income inside, it's helpful to purchase the correct insurance. You may want to consider Medigap to cover services your Original Medicare does not cover. You need to check the plans carefully before signing up, as not all plans cover the same things. Conversely, you could choose to enroll in Medicare Advantage, which covers more services than Original Medicare. Remember that you cannot use Medical Advantage and Medigap at the same time. Finally, you should consider whether you want to invest in long-term care insurance. This insurance will cover your needs if you ever need a home health aide or to reside permanently in an assisted living or nursing home—some of the few things that Medicare does not cover.

Now that you have a clear understanding of your options for saving money on healthcare, let's look together at another important aspect of retirement planning: your government pension. Make sure to check out the next chapter when you're ready to learn about pensions!

8

THE GOLDEN YEARS - UNDERSTANDING YOUR GOVERNMENT PENSIONS

Retirement is wonderful if you have two essentials: much to live on and much to live for.

— UNKNOWN SOURCE

Throughout this book, we've been talking about retirement planning as your key to creating the life of your dreams. We've already talked about how to use Social Security and Medicare to help you achieve that ideal life. Now we're going to talk about government pensions.

WHAT ARE GOVERNMENT PENSIONS?

Government pensions are retirement plans set up for all federal employees. If you worked for any branch of the federal government, no matter what your job was, you are entitled to benefits under the Federal Employee Retirement System (FERS).

FERS covers all federal employees, regardless of what branch you worked in. So, if you were a receptionist for a legislator, a federal prosecutor, or were on the White House staff, you're covered. However, it does not cover military personnel or non-federal employees. Public school teachers, for example, are considered government employees, but at the state or local level, so they would not receive FERS benefits.

There are three types of benefits via FERS: the Basic Benefit Plan; Social Security; and the Thrift Savings Plan. The Basic Benefit Plan is likely what you are thinking of when you consider the idea of a government pension. This plan is a "defined benefit plan," which means it offers you a set amount of income per month, based on how much you made while you were working. It is calculated using the length of time you were employed by a federal employer and your three highest years of earnings. The Basic Benefit Plan doesn't take into account things like overtime or bonuses; it just looks at your base salary for the three highest-paid years.

To calculate the pension amount, the agency multiplies the average salary (using the high-three data) by the years of service, then multiplies that by one percent. For example, if you worked for 25 years and your average salary was $65,000/year, your annual pension amount would equal 25 x $65,000 x .01, or $16,250/year. This would then be divided by 12 to give you a monthly pension payment of $1,354.17. If you are over the age of 62, and have been in service for, at least, 20 years, your multiplier rate is 1.1 percent instead of 1 percent. Using the example above, you would get $17,875 per year or $1,489.58 per month.

Although some government pension plans cancel out Social Security, FERS is not one of them. Federal employers pay Social Security tax on your earnings. Thus, you are entitled to the same Social Security retirement benefit as private employees.

The Thrift Savings Plan, or TSP, is similar to a 401k. Your employer automatically deposits one percent of each paycheck into your TSP and you can voluntarily contribute more than that. Contributions are tax-deferred. Unlike Social Security or your Basic Benefit Plan, your TSP is a "defined contribution plan." This means that you are required to make contributions to the plan, but it doesn't offer you a set amount each month. You will receive a list of potential investments when you set up your TSP and must choose where to invest your funds. The amount in your account at any given time depends on the investments you've made, and you can lose money if you are not careful.

There are various types of retirement benefits that you can take as a government employee. You can receive full retirement benefits if you are disabled; you can also take early retirement, beginning at age 57. You may also be entitled to benefits if you are laid off from your job.

To begin receiving benefits, you need to file an application with the Office of Personnel Management (OPM). It's best to apply about two months before retirement.

There are various types of government pensions. Social Security retirement benefits are a government pension. So are any funds you receive from your state or local government as a retirement benefit.

FERS pension eligibility requirements are similar as those for Social Security retirement benefits. However, federal employees become eligible for full retirement at 57, whereas you do not become eligible for any Social Security retirement benefits until your 62nd birthday, and are further not able to claim full retirement benefits unless you wait until you are 67. When we discuss FERS eligibility at age 57, we mean only that you are able to receive any money from the program. Your FERS benefits are the money you receive each month once your application is processed.

MANAGING YOUR PENSION AMONG OTHER INCOME SOURCES

As a retiree, it's important to manage all your income appropriately so that you continue to pay your living expenses, save money for emergencies, and continue doing things you enjoy with whatever's left over. Managing your money, as a retiree, is not that different from managing it during your working years, but there are some special considerations.

There are several types of budgets you might want to consider:

- **The envelope method:** This type of budgeting requires you to create an envelope for each type of expense you anticipate. For example, you might have envelopes for rent, food, clothing, and so on. You then withdraw the amount of cash you have budgeted for each category and place it in the appropriate envelope. When the cash in an envelope is gone, you cannot spend any more in that category. This method is very tactile—you feel the money in your hand and see the amount in each envelope go down over the course of the month. However, it requires you to use cash for all purchases, which may not be feasible. For example, your landlord may not accept cash for rent payments. However, if a vendor who does not accept cash accepts cashier's checks or money orders, you could convert the requisite amount of cash to one of these instruments.

- **The zero-budget method:** While using this method, income and expenses must be perfectly balanced, meaning that after you complete your plan, you should have a balance of $0 that is not accounted for. If you find you have extra money after listing all your expenses, you must decide what to do with it. You can allocate it to a combination of savings, spending, and donations to charity, but you must account for all money so that you don't mindlessly spend your surplus without forethought.

- **The ratio method:** This method requires you to allocate a certain percentage of your income to savings and a certain amount to discretionary spending, with the rest allocated for expenses. This method encourages you to "pay yourself first" by transferring money to your savings account and putting money aside for discretionary spending before you pay your bills. It's important to ensure that you leave enough money to cover your expenses if you use this method; you may have to adjust the percentage of your income that "you pay yourself" to ensure your bills are paid.

Whatever budget method you use, you should strive to save three to six months' worth of income in your emergency savings fund, so that you have enough to keep you afloat should you experience a major hit to your finances, such as the loss of a job.

Once you have sufficient money saved, it's a good idea to pay off any debts you still owe, such as student loans or balances on your credit cards. Paying back debt often takes significant time, but it can free up money in the long run. If you can afford to do so, you should pay more than the minimum required payment so that you can pay off your debt sooner and pay less in interest. This is especially important for retirees. Not only will you have more disposable income if you pay off your debt, but you will also protect your heirs—your estate's debts must be paid before any inheritances can be distributed from what is left over.

Some people also invest excess money once they are debt-free and have a secure financial foundation. If you have a 401k, you are already making choices about how to invest your savings; in addition, if you learn how to invest wisely or hire a financial planner to help you, you might be able to create a nest egg for your children and grandchildren.

Retirees can also employ some of the following special strategies to manage their finances:

- **Delay claiming your Social Security benefits for as long as possible.** The longer you wait, the more money you will receive each month after you begin collecting.
- **Create a separate account for your healthcare costs.** You may have greater healthcare needs as you get older, and Medicare won't cover everything. Saving money in a separate account for healthcare can help defray the costs. You might also want to consider enrolling in a medical savings account.
- **Analyze your home equity.** Knowing how much equity you have in your home can help you plan your finances. If needed, you can take a loan out against your home equity

line of credit (but make sure you pay it back in a timely manner!).

- **Consider downsizing.** If you own your home outright, selling it and moving to a smaller place might be a wise financial move. Many older people purchase a condo or move to a rental unit, especially if your partner has passed away and your kids no longer live with you. If you don't need so much space, downsizing may make both emotional and financial sense.

MEET GEORGE

George has served his country his entire adult life. After 15 years of exemplary service to the military, he shifted gears and got a job in the public sector so that he could continue to be of service as a civilian. He remained at his job for over three decades, retiring at the age of 63.

Once George retired, he felt lost and confused for the first time in his life. He knew he was entitled to two pensions from his two careers, but he wasn't sure how to get the maximum benefit or how to begin receiving them. He also had begun contributing to a Roth IRA when he was in the military and had some investment income.

Working with a financial advisor helped George figure it all out. His financial planner examined his pensions and explained how they were calculated, and how and when to request to receive them. He learned that it made financial sense to request his military pension immediately, as the amount wouldn't change if he deferred reception, but that he should delay getting his civilian pension to receive larger benefits later, and that he could use his retirement savings and investment income to help him pay his bills in the meantime.

By being willing to ask for help, learning about his different income sources, and creating a concrete plan, George has ensured the best financial outcome possible for his retirement.

PENSION CHECKLIST

Here's what you need to do to maximize your pension benefits. Check off each item as it is completed.

- Learn what pensions you may be entitled to. You may be able to get this information online, by speaking to someone who works in the appropriate department, or by speaking to your financial planner.
- Learn the benefit amounts you are entitled to, and whether any benefits will grow larger over time so that you can decide when to claim your pension.
- Before applying for a pension, gather all necessary documents, such as your birth certificate, documentation of who is in your family, proof of years of service, proof of any name change, any certificates of death or divorce (needed to prove you are no longer living with the partner you were with at your time of service), and any required endorsements or recommendations. You may need to get certified copies of some documents if they must be attached to your application form or if you don't have the originals.
- Fill out your application for pension and attach copies of necessary documents.

- Communicate, as needed, with the department handling your pension to make sure your application is processed correctly and you get the correct amount owed to you each month.

SUMMARY

If you are a current or former federal employee, you must have a solid understanding of government pensions.

Federal employees are entitled to a government pension (except for military personnel, who receive pensions under their own system). This pension supplements your Social Security retirement benefit; it does not replace it. Thus, you need to understand the different rules governing government and Social Security retirement benefits. For instance, it's possible to retire from government service at an earlier age than when you become eligible to receive Social Security benefits. If you are a state employee, such as a public-school teacher, you will receive a state pension, which may be governed by different rules from federal pensions.

In any case, it's important to understand when you become eligible for a pension and how your benefits are calculated. You also need to manage your retirement income, including pensions, so that you can save money for emergencies, pay off any debt you owe, and have money available for the type of experiences you want to have during your retirement.

To drive the point home, consider the anecdote about George, the military and civil servant described in this chapter. George was confused about his pension benefits prior to speaking to a financial planner; his willingness to seek help and be proactive about managing his retirement income allowed him to develop a plan, thus maximizing his benefits.

The checklist at the end of the chapter is designed to help you get ready to claim your pension. Government pensions are only one part of retirement planning. In the next chapter, we will go into more detail about how to plan your finances before and during retirement.

9

SECURING YOUR RETIREMENT - BUILDING A FINANCIAL FORTRESS

Nearly 46% of retirees leave the workplace earlier than planned because of some illness or job loss (Employment Benefit Research Institute, 2023). The COVID pandemic accelerated this problem; many people lost their jobs or chose not to return to them because of fear of illness, which made their lives more difficult because they didn't have the financial security they needed.

Don't let something similar happen to you. You never know when something might happen that leaves you jobless. But if you've planned for retirement correctly, you'll have money in your emergency fund and retirement savings account to tide you over until you put the rest of your plan into place.

In this chapter, we'll talk about all the components of retirement planning and how to ensure that you have the financial stability to retire even if unexpected events throw a monkey wrench into your plans.

WHAT IS RETIREMENT PLANNING?

Don't let the words scare you. Retirement planning simply means deciding how you will support yourself and your family financially after you retire, and how you will ensure you have enough money to retire comfortably.

Retirement planning often includes things like:

- How long you will continue working—you may need to work until you are 67 or older to ensure you maximize your Social Security benefits and put enough money in your retirement account to be able to afford your post-retirement goals.
- Deciding when to claim Social Security retirement benefits and other pensions. In earlier chapters, we discussed the benefits of delaying your claims; remember, each individual or family's circumstances are different, so you'll need to make the choice that is right for you.
- Understanding what sources of income will be available to you post-retirement and planning your finances accordingly.
- Seeing what expenses you will have after retirement and deciding whether to cut back on some of them.
- Planning for how to cover current and anticipated healthcare costs.
- Determining whether your retirement goals are feasible and what you need to do to reach them.
- Saving money while you are still working so that you will have it when you retire.

The earlier you can begin retirement planning, the better. Retirement savings grow over time if you or your financial planner make good investments, so if you start early, you'll build a bigger nest egg than if you wait until later. However, it's never too late! Even if you are near your retirement age, it's better to start saving now than to not do it at all. Retirement planning might not sound like much fun, but you'll be glad you did it after you retire and are able to enjoy yourself... thanks to your careful planning.

STEPS TO CONSIDER

Everyone's retirement plan looks slightly different. But in general, there are a few steps you want to consider. However, before you create any other plan, decide how much money you will need for your retirement. This will give you a savings goal to work toward as well as help you understand what it'll take to make your dream a reality.

Think about the various things you want to do and find out how much they cost on average. Don't forget to consider your living expenses, too—you'll still need to be able to pay for food, shelter, and transportation after you retire. You may want to budget a little more for these than you currently pay to take possible inflation into account. If this is too overwhelming, you can also use a formula to help you decide how much to save. Many people set a goal of putting 12 years of pre-retirement income away; others like the idea of their expenses adding up to no more than four percent of their retirement savings each year (Investopedia, 2023).

Depending on your life circumstances, you might need to consider certain factors when thinking about how much money you need to save:

- **Do you have children or grandchildren, or are you expecting some in the future?** New generations come with extra expenses. If you have adult children who are planning their own families, keep in mind that you may want to give gifts to your future grandchildren or pay for things for them that their parents couldn't ordinarily afford. These extra expenses will affect how much you need to save for your retirement.

- **What are your plans for retirement?** If you want to travel, you'll have different expenses than someone who wants to stay at home. If you're planning on selling your house and moving into a retirement community, consider how that will affect your finances.

- **Do you have your family nearby?** If you have no ties to your local community, you might consider moving to a cheaper city or even to another country with a lower cost of living.

- **What taxes will you have to pay?** Talk with your accountant or financial planner to find out the tax consequences of withdrawing money from your retirement accounts.

Once you understand your expenses and financial needs, the next step is to understand your "time horizon." In other words, how much time do you have to save this money? If you have 30 years before you reach retirement age, you can save at a slower pace than someone who first starts saving at the age of 60.

In addition, if you have lots of time. you can afford to take bigger risks with your retirement savings. Most retirement accounts, such as IRAs or 401(k)s, grow your money by investing it in stocks, bonds, or mutual funds. You decide which vehicles to invest your funds in; if you have lots of time to save, you might choose higher-risk investments with possibly higher returns than if you'll need the money fairly soon, as you will have time to recoup your losses. You'll also want to consider inflation and ensure your returns outpace it. The closer to retirement you are, the more secure your investments should be. You'll need the money soon, so focus on keeping as much of it as possible and on stable investments, such as bonds, that may grow at a slower rate, but guarantee excellent returns.

Don't assume your expenses will be less when you retire. That's often not the case—you can't anticipate healthcare costs, expenses related to grandchildren who have not yet been born, or changes to the economy, after you retire. Make sure you budget with the idea that your expenses will be comparable to what you are spending now, if not higher. In addition, consider your potential longevity. Your health and the age your parents lived to can help you predict how long you are likely to live. This is important because someone who expects to live into their 90s, or beyond, will need their retirement savings for far longer than someone with a life expectancy of 75 or 80.

ESTATE PLANNING IS ALSO IMPORTANT

In addition to planning your post-retirement life, you'll need to make some decisions about what you want to happen to your assets after your death. You'll need the help of a lawyer for estate planning. Your lawyer can draft a will and advise you as to the tax implications of various types of bequeathments. That way, you can ensure that you leave your heirs with extra money and not a big tax burden.

You'll also want to consider life insurance as part of your estate planning. Life insurance will provide your beneficiaries with some money after your death, which will help with funeral costs.

KEY FACTORS IN RETIREMENT PLANNING

There are four key factors you must consider in your retirement planning.

- **Inflation:** It is important to consider inflation because it can seriously damage your retirement savings' ability to cover your expenses. A three percent inflation rate might not seem like much, but $100 today will only be worth $34.44 after 30 years! To counteract this, ensure your retirement vehicles offer a growth rate that outpaces inflation.
- **Taxes:** Taxes can be complicated when it comes to retirement. You may have to pay taxes on withdrawals from retirement savings, and if your Social Security benefits cause you to take in more than $25,000/year ($32,000 for married couples filing jointly), you will have to pay taxes on those benefits as well. There are also tax considerations in play when saving for retirement. For example, contributions to your retirement income are tax-deferred, which means that you don't pay payroll taxes on them, but they also can't be used, which may leave you with less money in your paycheck.
- **Compound interest:** It is something that helps your money grow. A thorough understanding of how it works will help you realize how much money you will have at retirement, if you put money away in various types of savings now. Compound interest is interest on both the

principal (your current balance) and prior contributions. Thus, the more consistently you deposit money in retirement savings, the more interest you will earn on your savings.

- **Personal savings:** They should be part of your retirement plan, too. Social Security retirement benefits aren't meant to cover all your expenses, so you'll need to have other sources of income during your retirement. And if you live a lot longer than expected, or discover you didn't save enough for your retirement, you might need to depend on personal savings to make up the difference. Make sure that you are saving regularly while working so that you'll have sufficient personal savings at and after retirement.

TOP WAYS TO PREPARE

If all this information about what you need to do feels overwhelming, take a deep breath. There are some steps you can take right now to ensure a successful retirement:

- **Start saving ASAP:** Ideally, you should save three to six months of income in your emergency savings so that if you're laid off or suffer some other financial crisis before your retirement, you have the money to cover for it. Keep saving every paycheck even after you reach this goal.
- **Figure out what your financial needs will be during retirement:** Make your retirement budget and set some savings goals for your personal and retirement accounts.
- **Contribute to the savings plan set up by your employer:** Begin making regular contributions to the 401(k) or other plan offered by your job. In many cases, your employer will match contributions, so you can save twice as much

for retirement if you arrange for a portion of your paycheck to be saved each pay period.

- **Talk to your employer about options:** If your employer doesn't currently offer a retirement savings plan, approach them about the possibility of starting one. Similarly, if your employer doesn't match your contributions, discuss the issue with them and see if it can be changed.

- **Save money in an individual retirement account (IRA):** In addition to your employer plan, put some money away for retirement in an IRA to increase your nest egg. There are different types of IRAs available with different rules, so be sure to talk to your financial advisor before opening an account.

- **Find out what kind of pension you'll be entitled to upon retirement:** Talk to your HR department or look online to read about pensions. It's helpful to know the eligibility requirements and whether there is any benefit to delaying your request to begin getting a pension after you retire from your job. Estimate the benefits you'll get from your pension so that you can include them in your retirement plan.

- **Learn how to invest wisely:** Study investment basics and learn about risks and returns, how to choose investments, and the different investment vehicles available. Understanding this can help you invest your retirement savings wisely. In addition, if you have enough extra income, consider investing some of it to increase the amount of money available to you in retirement.

- **Leave your retirement savings alone until after you reach retirement age:** Not only are there penalties for early withdrawal, but the money won't be there when you need it if you withdraw it now! Find some other ways to handle emergencies, such as using emergency savings, taking out a bank loan, or using credit cards with low interest rates. If you find you are regularly scrambling for money, examine your budget closely and cut expenses so that your retirement savings can stay where they belong until you retire.

- **Ask questions:** Hire a financial planner to assist you with your retirement planning—but don't sit back and let them do everything. Ask questions to ensure you understand your options and the reason behind the planner's advice before consenting to their plan.

BALANCING VARIOUS SOURCES OF RETIREMENT INCOME

A key part of your retirement planning is understanding how the various sources of retirement income work together.

After retirement, you may have many sources of income:

- Social Security retirement benefits
- State or federal pension if you worked a government job
- Military pension, if you served
- Private pension from any private employer
- Withdrawals from retirement accounts
- Paychecks from any jobs you take post-retirement

It can be confusing to figure out how much money you're getting, what money comes when, and how much to take from your retirement savings. The best way to balance these things is to use the tips in the above section to prepare for retirement. Specifically, you need to understand how much you will get from Social Security, which varies depending on when you choose to take it; how much you will get from any public or private pension; and how much you plan to withdraw from retirement savings each month.

This is where hiring a financial planner comes in handy. Choose someone who understands retirement planning and who will work with you to set and achieve financial goals for your retirement. Your financial planner can help guide your savings and investment strategy while you are still working, go over options for when to claim pensions and other retirement benefits so that you get the maximum benefits due, and help you create a withdrawal strategy for your retirement savings that will allow them to last as long as possible.

Remember George, the hypothetical retiree we met in Chapter 7? Let's look together at how he approaches his retirement planning to help you understand the process better.

- George learned he was entitled to a military pension. With the help of his financial planner, he discovered that he was entitled to 2.5% of his final monthly pay for every year of service. Since he served for 15 years, he is entitled to 37.5% of his final monthly pay (to calculate this, he multiplied 2.5 X 15). He also learned that there was no advantage to delaying his claim for these benefits, and took them as soon as he retired.
- George was also entitled to a civil pension for his job in the public sector, which he worked at for 30 years. Since this pension is calculated based on the average of his three highest annual salaries, he remained with this job longer than originally planned to maximize his benefits, while simultaneously getting his military pension. He was also careful to take as few sick days as possible during his final

three years of work, as unused sick leave is added to the pension calculation.

- George asked his financial planner if he was allowed to take both pensions at the same time. He learned that he was, but there was a caveat: he could not get two pensions for the same year. In other words, he could not ask for his years of military service to be counted toward his federal pension amount unless he waived his right to his military service pension. After going over his options, George decided the best thing to do was ask the federal government not to count his military service when calculating his federal pension. That way, he could draw both pensions, which would give him more money per month than if he rolled them both into his FERS pension.

- Next, George had to decide what to do with his Social Security benefits. George's wife had passed away, so he was entitled to survivor benefits, which he would have to give up to claim his retirement benefits. He was still in good health and able to work when he turned 62, so he decided to continue getting his survivor benefits and delay getting his retirement benefits until later in order to get more of his retirement benefits. He re-evaluated at age 67. He could have delayed his benefits until age 70 to get the maximum amount, but he was beginning to get fatigued and had recently been diagnosed with diabetes, so he decided to retire from his job. However, he had rental income from some real estate investments coming in as well as his pensions, so he did not need to take his Social Security benefit until age 70, which gave him the maximum benefit.

- George had retirement savings from both a 401(k) and Roth IRA, and discussed with his financial planner how best to use these savings, taking into account that he was likely to live into his late 80s, based on his health and his family history. He also had a year's worth of income saved in his emergency savings as a backup. He also had a life insurance policy that he had purchased when he was in the military.

- After he turned 65, George enrolled in Medicare Part A, but kept his VA insurance for other types of medical treatment. However, after his diabetes diagnosis at age 67, he examined his options and decided that Medicare Advantage gave him the best coverage for his healthcare needs and switched his Medicare insurance to that program.
- George's grandson was born soon after his retirement, so George consulted his attorney about updating his will to ensure his grandson would be provided for after his death.

RETIREMENT BUCKET STRATEGY

One popular strategy for retirement planning is the bucket strategy. This is an investment strategy that takes all of your needs into account by considering:

- immediate cash needs
- intermediate needs (e.g., you'll need the money in the near future)
- long-term needs, such as saving for retirement years in the future

The idea behind this strategy is to help you create long-term investments with your retirement funds that you need by also attending to your immediate and short-term needs, so that you don't have to quickly sell off investments to gain cash.

To use this strategy, you'll need to invest in a variety of instruments. You can use certificates of deposit, high-yield savings accounts, and Treasury bonds; these are all liquid investments that can easily be converted to cash. You'll want two years' worth of income to be tied up in these types of investments so that you can have peace of mind that your immediate needs will always be covered. For example, if you need to pay $50,000/year in expenses after retirement, you should have $100,000 worth of investments in this bucket.

Your intermediate bucket should give you access to funds to cover years 3 through 10 of retirement. You'll also want some long-term investment vehicles such as preferred stock options, longer-term bonds, and utility stocks. Finally, your long-term investments should include riskier assets that may lose money in the short term and gain it in the longer term.

If you are not well-versed in different types of investments, your financial planner can help you understand your options and create a portfolio that includes all three buckets. One type of investment you might want to consider is a Treasury Inflation-Protected Security bond (TIPS). This bond is protected against inflation, which means that the value of the bond rises when inflation occurs. This ensures that the bonds are worth the same amount when cashed in as they would be if inflation rates had not made money worth less over time. For example, if inflation causes a dollar in 2023 to be worth only 70 cents, TIPS bonds will rise in value to account for the change.

STAYING INFORMED ABOUT POLICY CHANGES

It's important to stay up-to-date about policies related to your Social Security retirement benefits and other types of retirement planning. Having the most up-to-date information can help ensure that you don't miss new deadlines and maximize your benefits.

One of the most important laws you should be aware of is the "Employee Retirement Income Security Act" (ERISA). First passed in 1974, this Act governs private employee retirement plans, spelling out eligibility requirements, protecting you against some losses, and requiring employers who offer retirement plans to fund them.

As of 2023, ERISA does not require any employer to provide a private retirement plan (Findlaw, 2020). However, it does require employers who do choose to offer such a plan to follow some guidelines. For example, employers who offer retirement plans must regularly provide employees with information about the plan, such as features and funding methods. It is not required to make all such information free of charge. Employers must also provide a minimum level of funding and have clear rules for how long an employee must work to become eligible for benefits after they retire. Fiduciaries are held accountable for some losses to retirement accounts under ERISA, and employees may sue if they don't receive the benefits they are entitled to.

ERISA applies to any retirement plan established after 1975.

There are several types of plans employers may provide under ERISA:

- **Defined benefit plans:** They provide you with a set monthly sum after retirement. For example, a plan that gives retirees $1000/month, or one that gives them five percent of their last year's salary each month, upon retirement would be a defined benefit plan.

- **Defined contribution plans:** These provide you with the balance in your account upon retirement. These types of plans often involve investing retirement funds, so it's possible you'll lose money if your investments don't pay off. 401k plans and profit-sharing plans are both defined contribution plans.

- **Money purchase plan:** It requires your employer to contribute a fixed amount to your individual account each year.

- **Simplified employee pension (SEP):** It is a type of employee pension plan that requires you to set up an Individual Retirement Account (IRA) and your employer to contribute regularly to it. Your employer contributes the lesser of 25% of your pay or $40,000 each year.

- **SIMPLE IRAs:** They are employer-matched contribution plans. Under these plans, employers match your contributions to your IRA. SIMPLE IRAs are for businesses that have less than 100 employees but make more than $5,000. This plan is meant to make retirement plans affordable for small businesses; employees can contribute up to $15,500 in 2023, while employers match contributions up to three percent of the employee's salary. Employers cannot offer a SIMPLE IRA if they sponsor other retirement plans.

- **Profit-sharing plans:** Also known as "stock bonus plans," they are defined contribution plans where each participant gets a certain percentage of the entire contribution to the plan. For example, if employees collectively contribute

$5,000 to the plan, each employee will get a small percentage of that contribution.

- **401k plans:** They are defined contribution plans in which you put away pre-tax dollars from each paycheck, which are then invested according to your directions. The money must stay in the account until you reach retirement age or separate from the employer (although some 401k plans are portable and can be transferred to a new employer). If you need the money before retirement, you can take a loan out against your 401k balance. In some cases, you may be able to withdraw funds in case of hardship, but remember: if you do that, you won't have them available when you retire.

- **Employee stock ownership plans (ESOPs):** They are defined contribution plans where the investments are primarily in employer stock. These types of plans are meant to encourage employees to own stock in the companies they work for.

The federal government oversees all of these plans; however, some types of employment are exempt from ERISA. Specifically, federal or state government jobs, jobs in churches or other houses of worship, and plans meant specifically to cover disability, unemployment, or workers' compensation are exempt. In addition, ERISA does not cover plans based in foreign countries for non-residents of the United States or unfunded excess benefit plans.

The Labor Department oversees eligible private pension plans, while the IRS ensures these plans are run in accordance with tax laws. The Pension Benefit Guaranty Corporation (PBGC), on the other hand, guarantees pension benefits if a defined benefit plan is terminated due to a lack of sufficient funds to pay retirees (Find-law, 2023).

MAKE YOUR BUDGET

To put what you've learned into action, make your first retirement budget. Use your favorite spreadsheet. On one side, record each planned type of retirement income, estimating how much per month you'll get:

- pensions
- Social Security retirement
- retirement savings
- other sources of income
- Use the spreadsheet to total your income.

Next, list all your expected expenses. Don't forget to consider things that may not have happened yet, such as new grandchildren or health issues that may arise later in life. Add up your expenses and have the spreadsheet also calculate your expenses minus your retirement income to see how much is left over.

Play around with the numbers, focusing especially on changing how much you have available per month from your retirement savings, and see how it makes your budget change. This will help you see what, and how, you need to save to achieve your financial goals.

SUMMARY

Retirement planning can be complicated, but it's very important. You need to know how much money you'll need to support your planned lifestyle after retirement, how much time you have to save for retirement, and what your options are for collecting retirement benefits and pensions once you retire. You also should consider estate planning, including making out your will and deciding what type of life insurance you need. Paying down debts will also aid in your estate planning, as you don't want your loved ones burdened with a lot of debt after you die.

It can be helpful to consult a financial planner to help you see how various aspects of your retirement plan can come together to create stable finances. For example, your financial planner can help you understand when the best time to take each of your pensions and your Social Security retirement is, how much you need to save for retirement, and how much to withdraw from retirement accounts each month after you retire. Finally, you will want to learn about investing and place retirement funds in various types of investments so that you have short-, medium-, and long-term investments to cover you during retirement.

Now with the hard part out of the way, we're almost done! In the next chapter, we'll explore how to implement your plan.

10

FROM PLANNING TO ACTION - PUTTING YOUR RETIREMENT PLAN INTO MOTION

Don't simply retire from something. Have something to retire to.

— HARRY EMERSON FOSDICK

Throughout this book, we've discussed the importance of retirement planning. Now, we're almost at the finish line— it's time to discuss putting our plan into action!

Applying for Social Security and Medicare

In order to get the benefits, you are entitled to, you must first apply for them. The application process can be confusing; so, here's what you need to know.

There are three ways to apply for Social Security and Medicare:

- Online
- Calling the national toll-free number: 1-800-772-1213 (TTY 1-800-325-0778)
- Visiting your local Social Security office

Before you apply, gather all the documents and information you will need:

- Documents about yourself and your family
- Your Social Security Number
- Any other Social Security number that you've used in the past
- Your date and place of birth
- Your citizenship status
- Whether you or anyone else has filed for Social Security on your behalf. If so, you'll need the Social Security number and name of the person who applied and the date of application
- The names and Social Security numbers of any spouses, including former or deceased spouses (if relevant, you'll also need their death certificate or your divorce decree)
- The names of any unmarried children under the age of 18, children between the ages of 18 and 19 who are still in secondary school, and children of any age who became disabled before the age of 22
- Certified copy of your birth certificate
- Bank or other financial institution's routing and accounting numbers
- The month you want retirement benefits to begin from, if you are applying for them

- Whether you want to enroll in Medicare Part B (only if you are within three months from turning 65)

Employment Documents

- The name and address of your employers for the last two years
- Your earnings for the last two years (if you apply between September and December, you will also need to provide an estimate of your next year's earnings)
- A copy of your Social Security statement (you can get this online)
- Beginning and end dates for active military service before 1968
- Information about whether, and when, you became unable to work due to illness or injury during the past 14 months
- Whether you or your spouse has ever worked for the railroad industry
- Whether you have earned any Social Security credits under a foreign country's system
- Whether you expect to earn a federal or state pension
- Photocopies of your W-2s or self-employment tax return

If you mail documents to the Social Security Administration, attach a cover letter with your Social Security number so that the SSA can more easily match the documents with your application. Your application for Social Security also entitles you to Medicare Part A; if you qualify for both, you will receive both. You need to separately apply for Medicare Part B through the Social Security office if you want to get this coverage.

If you are younger than 65 and have ESRD, you can apply for Medicare via telephone by calling **1-800-772-1213** (TTY **1-800-325-0778**).

If you are applying for a government pension, this requires a separate application. Obtain the application through your employer or union about six months before you intend to start collecting it. You will need most of the same documents you need for Social Security to apply for a government pension.

SEEKING PROFESSIONAL ADVICE

Throughout the book, we've discussed the possibility of getting help from a financial advisor or planner. It's important to ensure you get the right advisor if you go this route; a financial planner or advisor who isn't familiar with retirement accounts and related issues might steer you in the wrong direction.

Retirement financial advisors help you plan and manage your finances both before and after retirement, but their main objective is to assist you with meeting your retirement goals. Your retirement financial advisor might be a certified public accountant, certified financial planner, or investment manager.

Retirement planners assist you in several ways, including:

- developing a budget and plan to save
- estate planning, including plans for long-term care (should it become necessary)
- investing money to increase your retirement portfolio
- minimizing tax liability

It's not mandatory to use a retirement planner, and many people don't. For some people, the cost can be prohibitive; others dislike the feeling of loss of control or being dependent on their financial advisor. However, using a financial planner can give you peace of mind or a place to turn to if you have any questions or concerns about your retirement plans.

It's important to ask questions and to work in partnership with your financial planner rather than allowing them to call all the shots. Remember: it's your money, and you are the one who will have to deal with the consequences if your planner makes poor investments or steers you in the wrong direction. Some financial advisors may try to sell you products or services they get commissions on, and it might not be in your best interest to buy these. Paying attention and asking relevant questions can help you avoid making mistakes when dealing with a financial planner.

TIPS FOR KEEPING TRACK OF YOUR PENSION

The most important thing you can do for yourself is keep records of how much your pension is supposed to be, and how much you get paid each month. That way, if there are any questions or discrepancies, you will have the documentation you need to get them resolved. You should also keep all your W-2s and paystubs (in case there are any questions).

Make sure you keep any information you are given about the rules of the plan so that you understand how much you need to contribute, how long you have to work, and what benefits you can expect to receive. Keep any benefits statements you get, and make sure to ask your plan administrator any questions that you may have. It's especially important to understand the rules governing the reduction of benefits.

Ask your plan manager for the plan's annual reports as well as look at its Form 5500 to see its current status. This will allow you to understand how the plan is funded and what the funding looks like. Find out whether you are entitled to "cost of living increases" in your benefits. Many plans do not offer this, which could significantly impact the funds you have available after retirement. Finally, you should ensure any former employers have your current contact information, in case they need to send the benefits to you or your beneficiaries.

WHAT IF MY PLAN IS TERMINATED?

If your plan is terminated, you will receive a notice 60 days in advance. You will need to find out whether a private insurance company or the PBGC is handling payouts to beneficiaries, as this will affect what you are able to get, and you will need to know who to contact with questions or concerns.

If your 401k is terminated, you will receive all benefits you are owed. If, for some reason, you don't, you can check with PBGC to see if they have any information. You can also look into whether your state is holding any unclaimed funds for you.

ACTION PLAN WORKSHEET

Let's plan your retirement together! Complete this worksheet.

- List total expenses after retirement: _____
- List sources of expected income: _____
- What date will I apply for Social Security and Medicare?
- What date will I apply for my pension(s)?
- What documents am I missing that I need?

- What information do I need about my private pension?

SUMMARY

Now that you know all about Social Security, Medicare, and pensions, it's time to plan your retirement. It's important to make sure you have all of your documentation available so that you can apply for Social Security and Medicare whenever you are ready. You will need information about yourself, your spouse, any former spouses, and your children, as well as information about your most recent work history and earnings. You will also need your statement of benefits from the Social Security office. Be sure to apply for Medicare Part B and D (or Medicare Part C) if you want the coverage, as it is not automatic. Medicare Part A may be.

You'll also want information about any private pensions or retirement plans you have participated in, especially about the type of plan you're enrolled in, how much you need to contribute, and what benefits you can expect. Most private pensions are covered under ERISA, and your employer is required to provide you with information about your eligibility and benefits.

Once you begin getting your pension, you should keep good records so that you can address it promptly if there is any type of discrepancy. If your pension is terminated by the pension holder, you have the right to benefits. Find out who is managing the benefit process after termination so that you know who to contact. If your 401k is terminated, you should immediately receive all of your benefits; if, for some reason, you don't, you'll have to contact the PBGC or the Labor Department to find out what happened to them.

You've come a long way! When you opened this book, you might have been confused or overwhelmed about retirement planning. Now you have a solid understanding of Social Security, Medicare, and pensions, and are equipped to plan the retirement of your dreams. The things we've talked about in this book aren't just theoretical; they're facts and ideas that light your path forward so that you can confidently move toward a financially independent and fulfilling retirement. Let's take a moment to reflect on the journey we've taken together.

Turn the page for some concluding thoughts.

Make It Easy for Someone Else

Life shouldn't be spent searching for answers to help us access what we're entitled to. Let's make it easy for more people to navigate the social security system and step into retirement calmly and confidently.

Simply by sharing your honest opinion of this book, you'll show new readers where they can find all the guidance they need to navigate the system and access the support they deserve.

WANT TO HELP OTHERS?

Thank you so much for your help. It makes a huge difference.

CONCLUSION

As you've learned throughout this book, retirement planning can be exciting when you know what you're doing.

The federal government wants everyone to have the same chance at a fulfilling retirement. Programs like Social Security and Medicare exist to ensure that you can live comfortably after you retire, and don't have to work longer than what is healthy for you. But these programs aren't automatic; you have to apply for them. Now that you've learned about the different options available to you, you can make a plan to do that, ensuring that you take full advantage of everything the government has to offer its retirees.

We've also discussed other aspects of your retirement planning, such as public and private pensions, and offered alternative Social Security programs for people who are not yet ready to retire but may have special needs. If you are a widow, divorcee, disabled person, or spouse who does not work outside the home, hopefully, you now understand all the benefits available to you.

Retirement planning involves a lot of moving parts, but you don't have to be overwhelmed while doing it. No matter how young or old you are, it's never too late to start creating the retirement plan that will give you the life you deserve. But don't stop there, though. Make sure you stay up-to-date on policies and programs that can help you and your family during this stage of your life. Subscribe to reputable retirement planning publications, talk with your financial advisor, and join retirement planning forums online so that you're always connected to the latest trends and won't be blindsided by economic surprises.

If you found this book helpful, please leave a review so that other people who are searching for answers to their questions about retirement can benefit from it, too.

Congratulations on your successful retirement!

REFERENCES

7 things to know about long-term care insurance. (2022, March 29). US Bank. https://www.usbank.com/financialiq/plan-your-future/health-and-wellness/costs-and-benefits-of-long-term-care-insurance.html

AARP. (2022, December 20). *How are Social Security disability benefits calculated?* https://www.aarp.org/retirement/social-security/info-2021/ssdi-benefit-calculation.html

Addressing healthcare costs of an aging population through digital transformation. (2023, June 16). Wolters Kluwer. https://www.wolterskluwer.com/en/expert-insights/addressing-healthcare-costs-of-an-aging-population-through-digital-transformation

Anderson, S. (2019, September 1). *A brief history of Medicare in America.* Medicare Resources. https://www.medicareresources.org/basic-medicare-information/brief-history-of-medicare/

Ball, R. M. (2020, October 13). *The nine guiding principles of social security: Where they came from, what they accomplish.* Social Security Works. https://socialsecurityworks.org/2020/10/13/nine-guiding-principles-of-social-security/

Fontinelle, A. (2023, February 19). *When to take Social Security: An overview.* Investopedia. https://www.investopedia.com/retirement/when-take-social-security-complete-guide/

Fonville, M. (2020, February 2). *9 reasons why retirement planning is important.* Covenant. https://www.covenantwealthadvisors.com/post/9-reasons-why-retirement-planning-is-important#:~:text=Retirement%20planning%20is%20important%20because

Chen, J. (2023, April 24). *Treasury Inflation-Protected Securities (TIPS) explained.* Investopedia. https://www.investopedia.com/terms/t/tips.asp#:~:text=Key%20Takeaways-

Daugherty, G. (2021, April 6). Early retirement: *The pros and (mostly) cons.* Investopedia. https://www.investopedia.com/articles/personal-finance/073114/pros-and-mostly-cons-early-retirement.asp#:~:text=Pros%20of%20retiring%20early%20include

Department of Labor. (2019). *Top 10 ways to prepare for retirement.* https://www.dol.gov/sites/dolgov/files/ebsa/about-ebsa/our-activities/resource-center/publications/top-10-ways-to-prepare-for-retirement.pdf

Dushi, I., Iams, H. M., & Trenkamp, B. (2017). The importance of Social Security benefits to the income of the aged population. *Social Security Bulletin, 77*(2), 1-12. https://www.ssa.gov/policy/docs/ssb/v77n2/v77n2p1.html

FindLaw. (2020, December 17). *Your retirement plan: What you should know.* https://www.findlaw.com/employment/wages-and-benefits/your-retirement-plan-what-you-should-know.html

Gigante, S. (2022, June 22). *Social Security filing strategies for the widowed.* MassMutual. https://blog.massmutual.com/retiring-investing/what-the-widowed-should-consider-when-filing-for-social-security

Hager, T. (2023, February 8). *Claiming Social Security benefits - early or late?* Forbes. https://www.forbes.com/sites/tomhager/2022/02/08/claiming-social-security-benefitsearly-or-late/?sh=33bf4642a984

Hayes, A. (2022, March 28). *Benefit-cost ratio (BCR): Definition, formula, and example.* Investopedia. https://www.investopedia.com/terms/b/bcr.asp

Huffman, L. (2023, January 13). *What is the retirement bucket strategy?* Smart Asset. https://smartasset.com/retirement/retirement-bucket-strategy

Investopedia. (2022, November 2). *How are Social Security benefits affected by your income?* https://www.investopedia.com/ask/answers/102714/how-are-social-security-benefits-affected-your-income.asp

Investopedia. (2023). *Pension plan definition.* https://www.investopedia.com/terms/p/pensionplan.asp

John Hancock. (n.d.). *Social Security's role in retirement planning.* https://www.johnhancock.com/ideas-insights/factoring-social-security-into-retirement-planning.html

Kagan, J. (2021, November 18). *5 key retirement planning steps to take.* Investopedia. https://www.investopedia.com/articles/retirement/11/5-steps-to-retirement-plan.asp

Kagan, J. (2022, March 25). *Employee retirement income security act (ERISA), history, purpose.* Investopedia. https://www.investopedia.com/terms/e/erisa.asp

Kagan, J. (2023, January 9). *What is retirement planning? Steps, stages, and what to consider.* Investopedia. https://www.investopedia.com/terms/r/retirement-planning.asp#:~:text=Retirement%20planning%20includes%20identifying%20income

Kagan, J. (2022, October 13). *What are Social Security benefits? Definition, types, and history.* Investopedia. https://www.investopedia.com/terms/s/social-security-benefits.asp

Key factors in retirement planning. (2023). Richwood Investment Advisors. https://www.richwoodia.com/key-factors-in-retirement-planning

Konish, L. (2022, November 1). *This social security quiz can help test how much you know about benefits before you claim.* CNBC. https://www.cnbc.com/2022/11/01/social-security-quiz-tests-how-much-you-know-about-benefits.html

Konish, L. (2023, February 1). *Wait until age 70 to claim Social Security: The return on being patient is huge, says economist.* CNBC. https://www.cnbc.com/2023/02/01/why-it-pays-to-wait-to-claim-social-security-retirement-benefits.html

Kurt, D. (2022, February 9). *Emergency fund.* Investopedia. https://www.investopedia.com/terms/e/emergency_fund.asp#:~:text=You%20establish%20an%20e-mergency%20fund

Learn how Medigap works. (n.d.). Medicare.Gov. https://www.medicare.gov/health-drug-plans/medigap/basics/how-medigap-works#:~:text=Medi-gap%20%26%20Medicare%20Advantage%20Plans

Lockett, E. (2021, January 15). *What are the advantages and disadvantages of Medicare Advantage plans?* Healthline. https://www.healthline.com/health/medicare/what-are-the-advantages-and-disadvantages-of-medicare-advantage-plans

Married couples have Social Security options. (n.d.). Vanguard. https://investor.vanguard.com/investor-resources-education/social-security/strategies-for-married-couples

McKenna, J. (2021, July 26). *Medicare Parts A, B, C, and D explained.* WebMD. https://www.webmd.com/health-insurance/medicare-21/medicare-parts-explained

Medicare. (n.d.). *How do I sign up for Medicare?* https://www.medicare.gov/basics/get-started-with-medicare/sign-up/how-do-i-sign-up-for-medicare

Medicare Interactive. (2019). *The parts of Medicare (A, B, C, D).* https://www.medicareinteractive.org/get-answers/medicare-basics/medicare-coverage-overview/original-medicare

Medicare Made Clear. (2023). *What is the difference between Original Medicare and Medicare Advantage?* United Healthcare. https://www.uhc.com/news-articles/medicare-articles/what-is-the-difference-between-original-medicare-and-medicare-advantage#:~:text=Medicare%20Advantage%20plans%20cover%20everything

Peck, B. (2023, February 4). *How to increase Social Security disability payments (7 ways).* Evans Disability. https://evansdisability.com/blog/how-to-increase-social-security-disability-payments/

Pension Rights Center. (2023, May 10). *Tips for keeping track of your pension: Additional detail.* https://pensionrights.org/resource/tips-for-keeping-track-of-your-pension-additional-detail/

Probasco, J. (2019). *9 ways to boost your Social Security benefits.* Investopedia. https://www.investopedia.com/articles/retirement/112116/10-social-security-secrets-could-boost-your-benefits.asp

Probasco, J. (2023, June 20). *How to manage income during retirement.* Investopedia. https://www.investopedia.com/retirement/how-to-manage-timing-and-sources-of-income-retirement/

Probasco, J. (2022, June 22). *Why do healthcare costs keep rising?* Investopedia. https://

www.investopedia.com/insurance/why-do-healthcare-costs-keep-rising/#:~:text=A%20Journal%20of%20the%20American

Promotion of sustainable employment - A. basic principles. (n.d.). International Social Security Association (ISSA). https://ww1.issa.int/guidelines/pse/174760

Ross, S. (2022, December 18). *Yes, you can manage your own retirement!* Investopedia. https://www.investopedia.com/articles/personal-finance/081715/yes-you-can-manage-your-own-retirement.asp#:~:text=Some%20good%20tips%20to%20manage

Rubin Law. (2013, October 3). *The Pickle Rule article.* https://www.rubinlaw.com/resources/the-pickle-rule-article/

Seladi-Schulman, J. (2021, May 28). Medicare and private insurance: Can you have both? Healthline. https://www.healthline.com/health/medicare/can-you-have-private-insurance-and-medicare

Social Security Administration. (2019). *Apply for disability benefits - child (under age 18).* https://www.ssa.gov/benefits/disability/apply-child.html

Social Security Administration. (n.d.). *Form SSA-1: Information you need to apply for retirement benefits or Medicare.* https://www.ssa.gov/forms/ssa-1.html

Social Security Administration. (n.d.). *Introduction to Social Security.* https://www.ssa.gov/section218training/basic_course_3.htm#:~:text=To%20provide%20for%20the%20material

Social Security Administration. (n.d.). *Social Security credits and benefit eligibility.* https://www.ssa.gov/benefits/retirement/planner/credits.html

Social Security Administration. (n.d.). *Social Security history.* https://www.ssa.gov/history/50ed.html#:~:text=Roosevelt%20signed%20the%20Social%20Security

Social Security Administration. (n.d.). *Social Security history - Ida May Fuller.* https://www.ssa.gov/history/imf.html

Social Security Administration. (2020). *Survivors benefits.* https://www.ssa.gov/benefits/survivors/

Substance Abuse and Mental Health Services Association. (n.d.). *Overview of Social Security disability programs: SSI and SSDI.* https://soarworks.samhsa.gov/article/overview-of-social-security-disability-programs-ssi-and-ssdi

Substance Abuse and Mental Health Services Association. (n.d.). *Social Security Administration programs for expediting disability claims.* https://soarworks.samhsa.gov/article/social-security-administration-programs-for-expediting-disability-claims

Substance Abuse and Mental Health Services Association. (n.d.). *SSI/SSDI and employment: A brief overview of SSA work incentives.* https://soarworks.samhsa.gov/article/ssissdi-and-employment-a-brief-overview-of-ssa-work-incentives

Tisdale, S. (2015, September 29). *Why your family is probably owed $120,000 in unclaimed social security benefits.* Black Enterprise. https://www.blackenterprise.

com/why-your-family-is-probably-owed-120000-in-unclaimed-social-secu rity-benefits/

Treece, D. D. (2023, June 7). *What to know before hiring a retirement financial advisor.* Forbes. https://www.forbes.com/advisor/investing/financial-advisor/what-to-know-before-hiring-a-retirement-financial-advisor/

Turner, T. (2022, August 17). *How to choose a Medicare plan.* RetireGuide. https://www.retireguide.com/medicare/compare/how-to-choose-a-plan/

What widows and widowers need to know about Social Security survivor benefits. (2020, October 13). Prudential. https://www.prudential.com/corporate-insights/widows-widowers-approaching-retirement-social-security-survivor-benefits

Whitelocks, S. (2015, January 30). *Meet Ida May Fuller, recipient of 1st Social Security check.* Daily Mail. https://www.dailymail.co.uk/news/article-2932568/Meet-Ida-May-Fuller-recipient-1st-Social-Security-check.html

You may be able to claim on your ex's earnings record. (n.d.). Vanguard. https://investor.vanguard.com/investor-resources-education/social-security/benefits-for-divorced-spouse

Your retirement readiness assessment in 31 questions: An action checklist to help you plan for your transition to retirement. (2005, January 1). ICMA. https://icma.org/docu ments/your-retirement-readiness-assessment-31-questions-action-checklist-help-you-plan-your-transition-retirement

www.ingramcontent.com/pod-product-compliance
Lightning Source LLC
Chambersburg PA
CBHW020354130626
46549CB00006B/2289